The
BLOOMING
of a LOTUS

The
BLOOMING

of a LOTUS

Guided Meditation Exercises for Healing & Transformation

THICH NHAT HANH

Translated by Annabel Laity

BEACON PRESS • BOSTON

Beacon Press
25 Beacon Street
Boston, Massachusetts 02108-2892

Beacon Press books
are published under the auspices of
the Unitarian Universalist Association of Congregations.

99 98 97 96 95   8 7 6 5 4 3

Text design by Christine Leonard Raquepaw

LIBRARY OF CONGRESS CATALOGING-IN-PUBLICATION DATA

Nhất Hanh, Thích.
    The blooming of a lotus : guided meditation exercises for healing
and transformation / Thich Nhat Hanh ; translated by Annabel Laity.
        p. cm.
    Translated from the Vietnamese.
    ISBN 0-8070-1222-X
    1. Meditation—Buddhism. I. Laity, Annabel. II. Title.
BQ5612.N47   1993
294.3'443—dc20   93-4191
                        CIP

CONTENTS

The function of meditation practice is to heal and transform. Meditation, as understood in my tradition of Buddhism, helps us to be whole, and to look deeply into ourselves and around us in order to realize what is really there. The energy that is used in meditation is mindfulness; to look deeply is to use mindfulness to light up the recesses of our mind, or to look into the heart of things in order to see their true nature. When mindfulness is present, meditation is present. Mindfulness helps us to understand the true essence of the object of meditation (whether it is a perception, an emotion, an action, a reaction, the presence of a person or object).

By looking deeply, the meditation practitioner gains insight, *prajñā*, or wisdom. This insight has the power to liberate us from our own suffering and bondage. In the meditation process, fetters are undone, internal blocks of suffering such as fear, anger, despair, and hatred are transformed, relationships with humans and nature become easier, freedom and joy penetrate. We become aware of what is inside us and around us; we are fresher, more alive in our daily existence. As we become freer and happier, we cease to act in ways that make others suffer, and we are able to bring about change around us and to help others become free.

The energy of mindfulness is constantly produced, nurtured, and strengthened during meditation. The meditation practitioner is like a lotus flower in the process of blooming. Buddhas are fully bloomed human flowers, beautiful and refreshing. All of us are buddhas to be. That is why in practice centers when people meet each other, they form a lotus with their palms and greet each other while bowing, saying: "a lotus for you, a buddha to be." As they inhale while saying "a lotus for you" and exhale, smiling, while saying "a buddha to be," they have the appearance of a blooming flower.

It may be possible for you to meditate on your own, without a teacher or a Sangha, namely, a Buddhist community of practice. But it goes without saying that to practice with a teacher and a Sangha is more advisable and much easier. A teacher is someone who has had the experience of the practice, and has succeeded in it. A Sangha is a meditation community where everyone follows more or less the same kind of practice. Since everyone is doing the same practice, it becomes easier for you to practice too, because the group energy emitted by the Sangha is strong and very supportive. You can also learn a great deal from individual members of the Sangha, especially those who have realized some degree of peace and transformation. There are many things you may find difficult to do when alone, but in the presence of the Sangha you can do them easily. All of us who have practiced with a Sangha can testify to this fact.

If you have no teacher or friends on the path, though, this

book may help you in the beginning. The subjects chosen for the meditation exercises in this book have been taken from the basic dhyana sutras of Source Buddhism and Mahayana Buddhism. The meditation taught in this book is the practice as perfected and taught by the Buddha. All of this book's exercises have been put into practice before being shared with the wider community of meditation students. Relying on the exercises of a practice that has been perfected, you may feel secure throughout the period of meditation. You need have no fear of beginning your practice right now, even if you have not yet had a chance to meet a teacher or find a Sangha.

In the Buddhist tradition, we consider Sangha one of the three gems. (The three gems are Buddha, Dharma, and Sangha.) As we see it, the three gems are already in your heart. The Sangha in yourself may guide you to the Sangha that is somewhere near you. Maybe the teacher and the Sangha are right there, very close to you, but you have not yet noticed. From the practice of the exercises in this book, you will generate the energy of mindfulness, which may lead you toward a teacher and a community. This book can be a mediator between you and a teacher, between you and a Sangha. Allow it to play its role.

Introduction

Meditation can be practiced almost anywhere—while sitting, walking, lying down, standing, even while working, drinking, and eating. Sitting is only the most familiar form of meditation, and the one we feel most privileged to enjoy, but there are many other forms that can be learned. During the past ten years, many thousands of people have come to Plum Village to practice meditation. From time to time, they have been offered guided exercises during sitting meditation sessions. At first, those who are used to sitting silently to meditate do not feel at ease during the exercises, but with practice they are able to experience the many benefits of guided meditation and consequently to experience transformation at a very fundamental level. Over the years, meditation students from many parts of the world have asked me to make these exercises more widely available.

The Subject Matter of the Guided Meditation

The guided meditations in this book have different purposes. Some exercises encourage joy within us; others enable us to discover our true nature, or help us heal, or shine the light of awareness in us, or release us from hurtful emotions. Some exercises have several purposes. The exercises that nourish and refresh our bodies and our minds should be done frequently. These exercises can be called the food of joy. (In the dhyana school, there is the expression "meditation as the food of joy," which means that the feeling of joy arising from the practice of meditation nourishes and sustains us. During the ceremony for offering rice at midday, we say, *"Receiving this food, we pray that everyone will be nourished by the enjoyment of the meditation practice and the enjoyment of the Dharma that will bring them to the realization of the full truth.")* Exercises one to four are especially suitable for this purpose. Such exercises connect us to elements that are refreshing and healthy, both in ourselves and in the world around us. They help us put an end to distracted thoughts, bringing us back to the present moment, to where we can recognize the oneness of body and mind. Although they are called nourishment exercises, they also restore internal balance, allowing the body as well as the mind to begin the work of healing. Other exercises help us renew contact not only with the self, the body, and the mind, but with the world at large, with family and society. We thus learn to overcome feelings of separation, loneliness, and isolation and begin to see a new way of being in, being part of, the world. Some of the exercises make us whole; and in others we learn to let go. Practitioners can judge from experience which exercises are most suitable for their needs and the circumstances in which they find themselves.

The Person Guiding the Meditation

Those who are chosen to guide sitting meditation exercises should be experienced in the practice of meditation; that is, they themselves should have realized an inner transformation. They should know how to invite[1] the bell during the meditation in a firm and unhurried way, so that the sound of the bell expresses and gives rise to a stable and calm state of mind. The voice of the guide should be neither too loud nor too soft. It should inspire and at the same time soothe. The guide must be sensitive to the needs of the participants. Just as the doctor must choose the medicine best suited to the patient, the guide must determine the most appropriate exercises for the community of participants. The subject matter of the guided meditation and the length of time allotted to it will be based on this understanding. If the participants experience delight and ease after each session of guided meditation, then the guide can be said to have succeeded in the task.

The Best Way to Practice

Before practicing any of the exercises, it is important to understand its purpose. Usually, the person leading a meditation will take five to seven minutes at the beginning of a session to explain the exercise. In this book you will find basic guidelines before each exercise. A single exercise can be practiced over several periods of meditation. After any session of guided practice, the person leading the meditation should be ready to hear the reactions of the par-

1. We never say "strike" the bell, because for us the bell is a friend who can wake us up to full understanding. We say "invite" the bell, meaning invite the bell to sound.

ticipants, so that in the succeeding sessions, the meditation can better fit their needs. Practitioners must be given enough time to grasp each stage of the meditation. For example, the in-breath is always accompanied by an image, and the out-breath often has another image, based on the preceding one. Using an image to meditate is much easier and more useful than using an abstract idea. The guide should allow as many as ten to twelve breaths, or even more, for the meditation participants to focus themselves. Indeed, every session should begin with a few minutes of mindful breathing so that participants can calm their minds and open themselves to the joy of meditation. The bell should not be invited with a full sound, lest it take the practitioners by surprise. The guide should simply wake the bell[2] before continuing on to the next stage of the exercise. The voice of the guide should be expressive of the spirit and the image upon which the participants are concentrating. This requires a little practice, and all participants should practice the role of guide so that at some time in the future they may be able to help others.

Breathing and Looking Deeply

Breathing and knowing that we are breathing is a basic practice. No one can be truly successful in the art of meditating without going through the door of breathing. To practice conscious breathing is to open the door to *stopping* and *looking deeply* in order to

2. To wake the bell means to touch it firmly with the inviter and not move the inviter away. This muffles the sound. A "wake-up" is always followed by an in-breath and an out-breath and then the full sound can be made. Making this full sound is called inviting the bell.

enter the domain of concentration and insight. The meditation master Tang Hoi, the first patriarch of the dhyana school in Vietnam (third century C.E.), said that "*Anapanasati* (being aware of the breathing) is the great vehicle offered by the Buddhas to living beings" (from the preface to the Anapanasmriti sutra). Conscious breathing is the way into any sort of meditative concentration. Conscious breathing also leads us to the basic realizations of the impermanence, emptiness, interdependent origination, selflessness, and nonduality of all that is. It is true that we can practice *stopping* and *looking deeply* without using conscious breathing, but conscious breathing is the safest and surest path we can follow. Thus all the exercises presented here employ the vehicle of conscious breathing. The breathing carries the image, and the image throws open the doors closed by our wrong perceptions.

"You only need to sit."

While practicing sitting meditation, you need to feel completely at ease. Every muscle in your body should be relaxed, including the muscles in your face. The best way to relax the muscles in your body is to smile gently as you breathe. You should keep your spinal column quite straight, but the body should not be rigid. This position will relax you and you can enjoy the feeling of ease. Do not make a great effort, do not struggle, do not fight. Let go of everything as you sit. This prevents backache, shoulder-ache, or headache. If you are able to find a cushion that fits your body well, you can sit for a long time without feeling tired.

Some people say they do not know what to do when they are sitting. They have been taught a correct meditation posture but do not know how to make their breathing light and even. The exercises found here will help them realize the oneness of body and mind. At the very least, they will learn that it is possible to do "something" while sitting.

"You only need to sit" is an exhortation of Tao Dong (Soto) meditation. It means that you should sit without waiting for a miracle—and that includes the miracle of enlightenment. If you sit always in expectation, you cannot be in contact with or enjoy the present moment, which always contains the whole of life. *Sit* in this context means to sit in an awakened way, in a relaxed way, with your mind awake, calm, and clear. Only this can be called *sitting,* and it takes training and practice.

Unfavorable Reactions to Guided Meditation

Some people find the sound of the bell and the spoken voice during the sitting meditation session disturbing. Accustomed to silence while meditating, they feel that their peace and joy is taken away from them in guided meditation. This is not difficult to understand. In silent meditation, you are able to calm your body and your mind. You do not want anyone to disturb that state of lightness, peace, and joy. But, if you are content only with this, you will not be able to go far in the work of transforming the depths of your consciousness. There are people who meditate only to forget the complications and problems of life, like rabbits crouching under a hedge to escape a hunter, or like people taking shelter in a cellar to avoid bombs. The feeling of security and protection arises naturally when we sit in meditation, but we cannot continue in this state forever. We need the vigor and strength to come out of the meditation hall into life, because that is the only way we can hope to change our world. In the practice of guided meditation, we have the opportunity to look deeply into the mind, to sow wholesome seeds there, to strengthen and cultivate those seeds so that they may become the means for transforming the suffering in us. Finally, we can also be guided in meditation to come face to face with that suffering in order to understand its root causes and be free of its bondage.

Guided meditation is not some new invention. It was used by practitioners in the time of the Buddha. This is clear if you read the Sutra for the Sick and the Dying (Ekottara Agama, chapter 51, sūtra 8; Madhyama Agama, sūtra 26; or Majjhima Nikaya, sutta 143). This sutra records the guided meditation that Sariputra used to help the layman Anathapindika when he was lying on his sick bed. The Venerable Sariputra guided Anathapindika step by step until he was able to transform his fear of death. The Anapanasati sutta is also a guided meditation teaching. In short, guided meditation has been part of the Buddhist tradition right from the beginning.

The guided meditation exercises in this book can help many practitioners by making their sitting meditation more concrete. Because of the systematic nature of the exercises, they could open a new era for the practice of sitting meditation.

The Breath, the Bell, the Guiding Sentences, and the Key Words

The leader of the guided meditation exercise first makes a "waking-up" sound on the rim of the bell to draw the attention of the community. She should allow five or six seconds to pass before reading the two guiding sentences. For example (from exercise four):

> Breathing in, I see myself as a flower.
> Breathing out, I feel fresh.

After that, she pronounces the *key words* (the condensed version of the guiding sentences):

> flower/fresh

A full sound of the bell signals the practice stage. After five, ten, fifteen, or more in/out breathings, the leader of the meditation invites another waking-up sound, allows five or six seconds to pass, and then reads the next two guiding sentences.

There are exercises where the in/out breathing is the sole object of mindfulness and concentration. For example (from exercise two):

> Breathing in, I know I am breathing in.
> Breathing out, I know I am breathing out.

In other exercises, the breathing carries in itself an image, and this image is visualized and kept alive during the whole in-breath or out-breath. The image is associated closely with the breathing. For example (from exercise four):

> Breathing in, I see myself as a mountain.
> Breathing out, I feel solid.

Breathing and Singing

Before beginning a Dharma talk or a Dharma discussion, it is always advisable to sit and breathe in accompaniment to music.

One person is chosen to sing and one person to play an instrument, and one person can guide the breathing of the Sangha. You can use the songs printed with the exercises. The person who guides the breathing can sit facing the community. She is like the conductor of an orchestra. As she breathes in, she draws her hand toward her heart (touching a place a little higher up than the physical heart is best). As she breathes out, she moves her hand away from her heart. The singer or the musician is watching her in order to keep the right tempo. If the audience is composed largely of children, the guide will breathe less slowly than for adults. If she is using the song "In, Out," when she draws her hand to her heart the singer will sing *in,* and when she moves her hand away the singer will sing *out.* When she draws her hand in again, the word *deep* will be sung; as she moves her hand away from her heart, the word *slow* is sung, and so on. With the song "Breathing In, Breathing Out," the words are naturally accompanied by the sign for breathing in and breathing out. Similarly, "I am blooming as the flower" is accompanied by an in-breath, "I am fresh as the dew" by an out-breath, and so on. As they listen to the singing, the whole Sangha will be breathing in unison. At the end of the song, they will follow their breathing in the same way, saying the words silently to themselves. At this point the words are not sung, but the tune can be played on an instrument. If no instrumentalist is available, the community practices in silence. The person guiding the breathing knows exactly how many in-breaths and out-breaths it will take to finish the song. After she has followed this number of breaths exactly, she signals to the singer to sing the song once again in the way described above. When this is done, all the practitioners will be very relaxed, and the community will be ready to begin the teachings or the discussion.

Guided Meditation Exercises

EXERCISE ONE

Joy of Meditation as Nourishment

1. Breathing in, I calm my body.   Calm
   Breathing out, I smile.   Smile

2. Breathing in, I dwell in the present   Present moment
   moment.
   Breathing out, I know it is a   Wonderful moment
   wonderful moment.

Many people begin to practice sitting meditation with the help of this exercise. Even those who have meditated for many years continue to practice it, because the exercise is so effective.

Breathing in, give complete attention to the in-breath. Wherever in the body the breath may be, feel the calm it brings. Just like drinking cool water on a hot day, feel how the breath cools the inner organs of the body. When practicing meditation, if the body is calm then the mind is calm. Conscious breathing makes the body and mind one. In breathing out, smile to relax all the facial muscles (the face has about three hundred small muscles in all). The nervous system will also be relaxed. The half smile can be seen as a sign of the calm brought by the in-breath, but it is itself also a means of attaining comfort and a clearer awareness of peace and joy. The conscious breathing and smile should be practiced during five, ten, or even fifteen in/out breaths before moving on to the second stage of the exercise.

Stage two of the exercise brings us back to the present moment. By dwelling in the present moment, we put an end to attachments to the past and anxieties about the future. Life is only available in the present. We need to return to *this* moment to be in touch with life as it really is. To know that we are alive, that we can be in contact with all the wonders within us and around us, this is truly a miracle. We need only to open our eyes and to listen carefully to enjoy life's richness. In using conscious breathing, we can transform the present moment into a moment full of wonder and beauty.

This exercise can be practiced anywhere at any time: in the meditation hall, in the kitchen, on the bank of a river, in a park; whether we are walking or standing still, lying down, or sitting; even when we are working.

EXERCISE TWO

Joy of Meditation as Nourishment

1. Breathing in, I know I am
   breathing in.
   Breathing out, I know I am
   breathing out.

   In

   Out

2. Breathing in, my breath grows deep.
   Breathing out, my breath goes slowly.

   Deep
   Slow

3. Aware of my body, I breathe in.
   Relaxing my body, I breathe out.

   Aware of body
   Relaxing body

4. Calming my body, I breathe in.
   Caring for my body, I breathe out.

   Calming body
   Caring for body

5. Smiling to my body, I breathe in.
   Easing my body, I breathe out.

   Smiling to body
   Easing body

6. Smiling to my body, I breathe in.
   Releasing the tensions in my body,
   I breathe out.

   Smiling to body
   Releasing tensions

7. Feeling joy (to be alive), I breathe in.   Feeling joy
   Feeling happy, I breathe out.   Feeling happy

8. Dwelling in the present moment,   Being present
   I breathe in.
   Enjoying the present moment,   Enjoying
   I breathe out.

9. Aware of my stable posture,   Stable posture
   I breathe in.
   Enjoying the stability, I breathe out.   Enjoying

8

While this exercise is easy and pleasant to practice, it also brings about many good results. Through this exercise, many people who are just beginning to meditate can taste the pure joy that meditation brings. Moreover, those who have already been practicing for some years can use this exercise to nourish body and mind and to continue further on the path of meditation.

The first stage (in, out) is to identify the breath. If this is an in-breath, the practitioner must know that it is an in-breath. If this is an out-breath, the practitioner must know that it is an out-breath. In concentrating on the breath even a few times, the practitioner will naturally stop thinking about the past and the future, putting an end to dispersed thoughts. This happens because the mind of the meditator is wholly with the breathing in its work of identifying the in-breath and the out-breath. In this way, the meditator has become one with the breathing. The mind is no longer an anxious mind or a thinking mind; it is simply a breathing mind.

The second stage (deep, slow) is to see that the in-breath is already growing deeper and the out-breath has already slowed down. This process happens of itself and does not require any effort on the part of the meditator. To breathe and to be aware that you are breathing (as in the first stage of the exercise) naturally makes the breathing deeper, slower, more even. In other words, the breathing has more quality. When the breathing has become even, calm, and rhythmical, the practitioner begins to feel peace and joy in body as well as in mind. The tranquillity of the breathing entails the tranquillity of the body and of the mind. At this point, the meditator begins to experience meditation as the food of joy.

The third stage (awareness of the whole body, relaxing the whole body) brings the mind home to the body with the in-breath, and mind becomes acquainted with the body. The breathing is the bridge that takes the meditator from the body to the mind and from the mind to the body. The function of the out-breath is to relax the whole body. While breathing out, the meditator allows the muscles in the shoulders, in the arms, and then in the whole body to relax, so that a feeling of comfort is apparent in the whole body. This stage should be practiced for at least ten in- and out-breaths.

The fourth stage (calming the body, caring for the body) calms the functions of the body with the in-breath. With the out-breath, the meditator expresses a heartfelt compassion for the needs of the body. If the meditator continues to practice the third stage, the breath will be utterly calming and help the meditator to treat the body with deep respect and care.

The fifth stage (smiling to the whole body, easing the body) brings relaxation to all the facial muscles. The meditator sends the half smile to the whole body, as if it were a fresh, cool stream of water. To ease the body is to feel light. This stage of the exercise nourishes the whole body through the compassion of the meditator.

The sixth stage (smiling to the body, releasing the tensions in the body) is a continuation of the fifth stage. Here the breathing helps remove all the tensions which still remain in the body.

The seventh stage (feeling joy, feeling happy) brings awareness of the feeling of joy when the meditator breathes in. This is the joy of being alive, of being in good health (which is the same as living in awareness), of being able to nourish the body at the same time as the soul. The out-breath brings a feeling of happiness. To sit with nothing to do but breathe in awareness is a great happiness. Countless people bounce about like yo-yos in their busy lives and never have the chance to taste this meditator's joy.

The eighth stage (present moment, wonderful moment) brings the meditator back to the present moment with the in-breath. The Buddha taught that the past has already gone and the future has not yet come; that we find life in what is happening *now*. To dwell in the present is truly to return to life. Only in the present moment is the meditator really in touch with the wonders of life. Peace, joy, liberation, the buddha nature, and nirvana cannot be found anywhere else. Happiness lies in the present moment. The in-breath helps the meditator be in touch with this happiness. The out-breath also brings much happiness to the meditator, and that is why he says, "wonderful moment."

The ninth stage (stable posture, enjoying) steadies the meditator in the sitting position he has adopted. It will help a posture which is not yet straight, not yet beautiful, to become both straight and beautiful. A stable sitting posture brings about ease and enjoyment of that stability. The meditator becomes master of his body and mind and is not pulled hither and thither by the different actions of body, speech, and mind, in which he might otherwise drown.

EXERCISE THREE

Joy of Meditation as Nourishment

1. Breathing in, I know I am
   breathing in.   In

   Breathing out, I know I am
   breathing out.   Out

2. Breathing in, my breath grows deep.   Deep
   Breathing out, my breath goes slowly. Slow

3. Breathing in, I feel calm.   Calm
   Breathing out, I feel ease.   Ease

4. Breathing in, I smile.   Smile
   Breathing out, I release.   Release

5. Dwelling in the present moment.   Present moment
   I know it is a wonderful moment.   Wonderful moment

This exercise also can be practiced anywhere, in the meditation hall, in the living room, in the kitchen, or while on a train.

The first stage is designed to bring body and mind back into oneness and at the same time to help bring us back to the present moment, to connect us with the miracle of life now occurring. If we can breathe in this spirit for two or three minutes, our breathing will quite naturally become light, leisurely, gentler, slower, and deeper, and naturally we shall feel much more at ease in body as well as in mind. This is the second stage, "deep, slow." We can stay with this stage for just as long as we like. Next we come to "calm, ease." Here we can achieve deeper tranquillity (Sanskrit *prasrabdhis*), a great calm of body and mind, and the joy of meditation will continue to nourish us. The final two stages have already been discussed in exercise two. We can learn by heart the gatha and we can also sing it.

In Out, Deep Slow

In, out. Deep, slow. Calm, ease. Smile, re-lease.

Pre-sent mo-ment. Won-der-ful mo-ment.

EXERCISE FOUR

Joy of Meditation as Nourishment

1. Breathing in, I know I am   In
   breathing in.
   Breathing out, I know I am   Out
   breathing out.

2. Breathing in, I see myself as a flower.   Flower
   Breathing out, I feel fresh.   Fresh

3. Breathing in, I see myself as a   Mountain
   mountain.
   Breathing out, I feel solid.   Solid

4. Breathing in, I see myself as still   Still water
   water.
   Breathing out, I reflect all that is.   Reflecting

5. Breathing in, I see myself as space.   Space
   Breathing out, I feel free.   Free

This exercise can be practiced in the first part of any period of sitting meditation, or for the whole of the meditation period, to nourish and calm body and mind, to enable the meditator to let go and attain freedom.

The first stage should be practiced for as long as it takes the body and mind to become one. The second stage encourages a sense of freshness. A human being should be as fresh as a flower, for indeed we are one species of flower in the garden of all phenomena. We only need to look at the beauty of children to see that human beings are flowers. Two round eyes are flowers. The clear complexion of the face with its gentle forehead is a flower. The two hands are a flower. . . . It is only because we worry that our foreheads become wrinkled. It is only because we cry so much and pass so many sleepless nights that our eyes are clouded. We breathe in to restore the flower in us. This in-breath brings the flower in us back to life. The out-breath helps us be aware that we have the capacity to be, and are now, fresh as a flower. This awareness waters our flower; this is the practice of loving-kindness meditation toward ourselves.

The third stage, "mountain, solid," helps us to stand firmly when we are upset by vehement feelings. Whenever we feel despair, anxiety, fear, or anger, we are carried right into the heart of a whirlwind. We are like a tree standing in the gale. If we look up, we shall see our branches bending as if they are about to break and be carried away by the storm. But if we look down, we shall know that the roots of the tree are held firmly in the earth, and we shall feel more stable and at rest.

Body and mind are like that. When there is a hurricane of emotions in us, if we know how to withdraw from the storm—that is, if we know how to withdraw from the turmoil of the brain—we shall not be swept away. We must transfer our attention to a place in the abdomen about two fingers' width below the navel and breathe deeply and slowly according to the formula "mountain, solid." In doing this, we shall see that we are not just our emotions. Emotions come and go, but we are always here. When we are oppressed by emotions, we feel very insecure and fragile; we may feel that we are in danger of losing life itself. Some people do not know how to deal with their strong emotions. When they are suffering greatly from despair, fear, or anger, they think the only way to put an end to their suffering is to put an end to their life. But those who know how to sit in a meditation position and practice breathing the exercise "mountain, solid," can weather such times of difficulty and suffering.

This exercise can be practiced lying down, resting easily on the back. Our entire attention should be directed to the rising and falling of the abdomen. This will enable us to leave the storm area and to know we need never go back there again. Nevertheless, we should not wait until we find ourselves in difficulty in order to practice. If we do not have the habit of practicing, we shall forget how to do the exercise, and our emotions may once again over-whelm and oppress us. To make a good habit, we should practice every day, in that way, whenever painful feelings arise we shall know quite naturally how to resolve and to transform them. In addition, we can explain the practice to young people to help them ride out their stormy periods.

"Still water, reflecting" is the fourth stage intended to calm the mind and body. In the Anapanasati sutta the Buddha taught: "Breathing in I make my mind calm . . ." This exercise is essen-tially the same, the image of the still lake water simply makes the practice easier. When our mind is not calm, our perceptions are usually clouded; what we see, hear, and think does not reflect the truth of things, just as when the surface of a lake is troubled by waves, it cannot clearly reflect the clouds above.

> Buddha is the cool moon,
> Crossing the sky of utter emptiness.
> The lake of the mind of beings quietens,
> The moon reflects beautifully in it.

Our sorrows, pains, and anger arise from our wrong perceptions. In order to avoid these wrong perceptions, we need to practice making the mind as still as the surface of a still lake. The breathing is what does that work.

"Space, free" is the fifth stage. If we have too many preoccupations and cares, we will not have clarity and peace and joy. Thus the purpose of this exercise is to create space for ourselves, space in our hearts and space around us. We must rid ourselves of the anxieties and projects that burden us. We should deal in the same way with sorrows and anger. We must practice letting go of the things we carry needlessly. This sort of baggage only makes life heavy, even if sometimes it seems we cannot be happy without it—without, for example, that a title, high position, fame, business, and people to run around after us). But if we look again, we shall see that this baggage is often nothing but an obstacle to our happiness. If we can just put it down, we shall have happiness. *"Buddha is the cool moon,/ Crossing the sky of utter emptiness . . ."* Limitless space is the sky of utter emptiness. That is why the happiness of the Buddha is so great. One day the Buddha was sitting in the forest at Vaisali and saw a farmer going past. The farmer asked the Buddha if he had seen his herd of cows, which had broken loose. He also said that earlier that year he had lost two acres of sesame fields when they were attacked by caterpillars and complained that he must be the most wretched person on earth. Perhaps, he said, he should put an end to his own life. The Buddha advised him to look in another direction. After the farmer had gone, the Buddha turned to the bhiksus who were sitting with him and smiled. He said: "Bhiksus, are you aware of your happiness and freedom? You do not have any cows you need be afraid of losing." Practicing this last exercise helps us to let go of our cows, the cows of our mind and cows we have gathered around us. It also can be sung:

Breath-ing in, breath-ing out. Breath-ing in, breath-ing

out. I am bloom-ing as a flow-er. I am fresh as the

dew. I am sol-id as a moun-tain. I am firm as the

earth. I am free.   Breath-ing in, breath-ing

out. Breath-ing in, breath-ing out.   I am wa-ter re -

flect - ing what is   real,   what is   true,   and I

feel   there is   space   deep in - side   of

me.   I am free,   I   am free, I   am   free.

EXERCISE FIVE

Taking Refuge

1. Breathing in, I go back to myself.
   Breathing out, I take refuge in my
   own island.

   Going back
   My own island

2. Breathing in, Buddha is my
   mindfulness.
   Breathing out, my mindfulness
   shines near and far.

   Buddha is
   mindfulness
   Shining near and
   far

3. Breathing in, Dharma is my
   conscious breath.
   Breathing out, the conscious breath
   protects my body and mind.

   Dharma is
   conscious breath
   Protecting body
   and mind

4. Breathing in, Sangha is my five
   skandhas.
   Breathing out, my skandhas
   practicing in harmony.

   Sangha is five
   skandhas
   Practicing in
   harmony

Although this exercise can be used anywhere and at any time, it is especially useful when we find ourselves in a state of anxiety and agitation and do not know what is best to do. It is a means of finding refuge through the Buddha, the Dharma, and the Sangha. When we practice this exercise, it takes us directly to a place of peace and stability, to the most calm and stable place we can go. Buddha taught: "Be an island unto yourself. You should take refuge in yourself and not in anything else." This island is right mindfulness, the awakened nature, the foundation of stability and calm that resides in each of us. This island is right teaching, which shines light on the path we are treading and helps us to see what we need to do and what we should not do. Finally, this island is also the Sanghakaya (community body). In each member of the Sanghakaya, the five skandhas, elements of body and mind, need to be in accord with each other. That is, our own skandhas must be in harmony before we can live in harmony with others. When the five skandhas are in harmony, then naturally there will be the right action that brings peace. We will find that the nervous system and heart rediscover their evenness and their calm. Conscious breathing itself brings about this evenness. If we can become aware that we are doing what is most appropriate in our moment of need, we shall see that we no longer have any reason to be anxious or agitated. Is there anything better we could possibly do than that? "Being an Island unto Myself" is a song to help us memorize the gatha:

Be - ing an is - land un - to my - self. As an

is - land un - to my - self. Bud - dha is my

mind-ful-ness. Shin-ing far, shin-ing near. Dhar-ma is my

breath-ing, guard-ing bo-dy and mind. I am free.

Be - ing an is - land un - to my - self. As an

is-land un-to my-self. San-gha is my skan-dhas, work-ing

in har-mo-ny. Tak-ing re-fuge in my-self. Com-ing

back to my - self. I am free, I am free, I am free.

Say you were on an airplane, and the pilot announced that the plane was in trouble and might crash, this exercise would enable you to calm yourself and to clear your mind. By bringing the Buddha, the Dharma, and the Sangha back to your own island to shine upon it, you would be able to find peace. If you were indeed to die, you would be able to die beautifully, as you have lived beautifully in mindfulness. You would have enough calm and clarity in that moment and would know exactly what to do and what not to do.

EXERCISE SIX

Touching, Connecting

1. Aware of the hair on my head,   Hair
   I breathe in.
   Smiling to the hair on my head,   Smiling
   I breathe out.

2. Aware of my eyes, I breathe in.   Eyes
   Smiling to my eyes, I breathe out. Smiling

3. Aware of my ears, I breathe in.   Ears
   Smiling to my ears, I breathe out. Smiling

4. Aware of my teeth, I breathe in.   Teeth
   Smiling to my teeth, I breathe out. Smiling

5. Aware of my smile, I breathe in.   Smile
   Smiling to my smile, I breathe out. Smiling

6. Aware of my shoulders, I breathe in. Shoulders
   Smiling to my shoulders,   Smiling
   I breathe out.

7. Aware of my arms, I breathe in.   Arms
   Smiling to my arms, I breathe out.   Smiling

8. Aware of my lungs, I breathe in.   Lungs
   Smiling to my lungs, I breathe out.   Smiling

9. Aware of my heart, I breathe in.   Heart
   Smiling to my heart, I breathe out.   Smiling

10. Aware of my liver, I breathe in.   Liver
    Smiling to my liver, I breathe out.   Smiling

11. Aware of my bowels, I breathe in.   Bowels
    Smiling to my bowels, I breathe out.   Smiling

12. Aware of my kidneys, I breathe in.   Kidneys
    Smiling to my kidneys, I breathe out.   Smiling

13. Aware of my feet, I breathe in.   Feet
    Smiling to my feet, I breathe out.   Smiling

14. Aware of my toes, I breathe in.   Toes
    Smiling to my toes, I breathe out.   Smiling

This exercise helps the meditation practitioner to become more attuned to her body. The in-breath is to touch a certain part of the body: eyes, ears, heart, lungs, and so on. The out-breath smiles to that part of the body. The half smile can soften and heal. It expresses care and affection for the body. The lungs, the heart, and the liver work diligently over many decades, but how often do we take the time to show them any attention and/or compassion? Not only do we fail to recognize when these parts of the body are tired and out of sorts, but we frequently treat them in a brutal way, weakening them even further. The liver is destroyed by drinking alcohol. Incorrect breathing weakens the lungs, makes them vulnerable to disease, and at the same time undermines the other organs of the body. If we are always anxious and worrying and over-emotional, if we eat too much fat, we can put our hearts at risk. But by breathing consciously and putting ourselves in touch with all the different parts of the body, we come to feel and understand the body and we learn in a concrete way how we can bring it peace and joy. The peace and joy of the body is nothing other than our own peace and joy. This exercise is an exercise of love meditation toward the body. If we are not able to love our bodies, then how can we love anyone?

The first time you practice this exercise you might think that it is too simple, but after you have been practicing it for some time, you shall see how important it is. At first you just recognize and smile to the different parts of your body, but gradually you shall see each individual part very clearly and deeply. Every hair and every cell contains all the data necessary to make the universe. That is the teaching of interdependence found in the Avatamsaka sutra. Every hair on your head is a message from the universe. You can realize awakening by meditating on a single hair.

If you are practicing on your own, you can use this exercise when you are lying down to relax or to go to sleep.

EXERCISE SEVEN

Touching, Healing

1. In touch with the air, I breathe in.   Touching air
   Smiling with the air, I breathe out.   Smiling

2. In touch with pure mountain air,   Pure mountain air
   I breathe in.
   Smiling with pure mountain air,   Smiling
   I breathe out.

3. In touch with pure countryside air,   Pure countryside
   I breathe in.   air
   Smiling with the countryside air,   Smiling
   I breathe out.

4. In touch with cool water, I breathe in.   Cool water
   Smiling with the cool water,   Smiling
   I breathe out.

5. In touch with the clear stream,   Clear Stream
   I breathe in.
   Smiling with the clear stream,   Smiling
   I breathe out.

6. In touch with the snow on the
   mountain, I breathe in.
   Smiling with the snow on the
   mountain, I breathe out.

   Snow on the
   mountain
   Smiling

7. In touch with the vast ocean,
   I breathe in.
   Smiling with the vast ocean,
   I breathe out.

   Vast ocean

   Smiling

8. In touch with the Arctic ice-fields,
   I breathe in.
   Smiling with the Arctic ice-fields,
   I breathe out.

   Arctic ice-fields

   Smiling

9. In touch with the clouds in the blue
   sky, I breathe in.
   Smiling with the clouds in the blue
   sky, I breathe out.

   Touching clouds

   Smiling

10. In touch with the sunshine,
    I breathe in.
    Smiling with the sunshine,
    I breathe out.

    Touching sunshine

    Smiling

11. In touch with the trees, I breathe in.
    Smiling with the trees, I breathe out.

    Touching trees
    Smiling

12. In touch with the children,
    I breathe in.
    Smiling with the children,
    I breathe out.

    Touching children

    Smiling

13. In touch with the people, I breathe in.
    Smiling with the people,
    I breathe out.

    Touching people
    Smiling

14. In touch with the singing of birds,
I breathe in.
Smiling with the singing birds,
I breathe out.

Singing birds

Smiling

15. In touch with the sky, I breathe in.
Smiling with the sky, I breathe out.

Touching sky
Smiling

16. In touch with the flowers,
I breathe in.
Smiling with the flowers,
I breathe out.

Touching flowers

Smiling

17. In touch with the spring, I breathe in.
Smiling with the spring,
I breathe out.

Touching spring
Smiling

18. In touch with the summer,
I breathe in.
Smiling with the summer,
I breathe out.

Touching summer

Smiling

19. In touch with the fall, I breathe in.
Smiling with the fall, I breathe out.

Touching fall
Smiling

EXERCISE EIGHT

Touching, Connecting

1. Aware of my eyes, I breathe in.
   Aware of light, I breathe out.

   Aware of eyes
   Aware of light

2. Aware of my ears, I breathe in.
   Aware of sound, I breathe out.

   Aware of ears
   Aware of sound

3. Aware of my ears, I breathe in.
   Aware of a cry of pain, I breathe out.

   Aware of ears
   Aware of cry of pain

4. Aware of my ears, I breathe in.
   Aware of singing, I breathe out.

   Aware of ears
   Aware of singing

5. Aware of my ears, I breathe in.
   Aware of the sound of rain, I breathe out.

   Aware of ears
   Aware of sound of rain

6. Aware of my ears, I breathe in.
   Aware of laughter, I breathe out.

   Aware of ears
   Aware of laughter

7. Aware of my ears, I breathe in.
   Aware of silence, I breathe out.

   Aware of ears
   Aware of silence

8. Aware of my skin, I breathe in.　　Aware of skin
Aware of the sense of touch,　　Aware of touch
I breathe out.

9. Aware of my skin, I breathe in.　　Aware of skin
Aware of the sun on my skin,　　Aware of sun
I breathe out.

10. Aware of my skin, I breathe in.　　Aware of skin
Aware of cool water on my skin,　　Aware of cool
I breathe out.　　water

11. Aware of my skin, I breathe in.　　Aware of skin
Aware of ice on my skin,　　Aware of ice
I breathe out.

12. Aware of my skin, I breathe in.　　Aware of skin
Aware of touching the bark of a tree,　　Touching bark
I breathe out.

13. Aware of my skin, I breathe in.　　Aware of skin
Aware of touching an earthworm,　　Touching
I breathe out.　　earthworm

14. Aware of my teeth, I breathe in.　　Aware of teeth
Aware of an apple, I breathe out.　　Aware of apple

15. Aware of my teeth, I breathe in.　　Aware of teeth
Aware of a toothache, I breathe out.　　Aware of toothache

16. Aware of my teeth, I breathe in.　　Aware of teeth
Aware of lemon juice, I breathe out.　　Aware of lemon
　　juice

17. Aware of my teeth, I breathe in.　　Aware of teeth
Aware of the dentist's drill,　　Aware of dentist's
I breathe out.　　drill

18. Aware of my tongue, I breathe in.
Aware of the taste of orange juice,
I breathe out.

Aware of tongue
Tasting orange
juice

19. Aware of my tongue, I breathe in.
Aware of the taste of lemon,
I breathe out.

Aware of tongue
Tasting lemon

20. Aware of my tongue, I breathe in.
Aware of the taste of salt water,
I breathe out.

Aware of tongue
Tasting salt water

21. Aware of my tongue, I breathe in.
Aware of the taste of hot pepper,
I breathe out.

Aware of tongue
Tasting hot pepper

22. Aware of my lungs, I breathe in.
Aware of smell, I breathe out.

Aware of lungs
Aware of smell

23. Aware of my lungs, I breathe in.
Aware of the scent of fresh grass,
I breathe out.

Aware of lungs
Smelling fresh
grass

24. Aware of my lungs, I breathe in.
Aware of the scent of roses,
I breathe out.

Aware of lungs
Smelling roses

25. Aware of my lungs, I breathe in.
Aware of the smell of dung,
I breathe out.

Aware of lungs
Smelling dung

26. Aware of my lungs, I breathe in.
Aware of tobacco smoke,
I breathe out.

Aware of lungs
Tobacco smoke

27. Aware of my lungs, I breathe in.
Aware of the smell of the sea,
I breathe out.

Aware of lungs
Smelling the sea

28. Aware of my liver, I breathe in.
    Aware of the taste of wine,
    I breathe out.

    Aware of liver
    Tasting wine

29. Aware of my liver, I breathe in.
    Aware of greasy food, I breathe out.

    Aware of liver
    Aware of greasy food

30. Aware of my liver, I breathe in.
    Aware of yellow skin caused by a
    sick liver, I breathe out.

    Aware of liver
    Aware of yellow skin

31. Aware of my feet, I breathe in.
    Aware of shoes, I breathe out.

    Aware of feet
    Aware of shoes

32. Aware of my feet, I breathe in.
    Aware of young grass, I breathe out.

    Aware of feet
    Young grass

33. Aware of my feet, I breathe in.
    Aware of sand on the beach,
    I breathe out.

    Aware of feet
    Sand on the beach

34. Aware of my feet, I breathe in.
    Aware of a thorn, I breathe out.

    Aware of feet
    Aware of thorn

35. Aware of my feet, I breathe in.
    Aware of an ant's hill, I breathe out.

    Aware of feet
    Aware of ant's hill

These two exercises help us to be in contact with wholesome and fresh things, which have the capacity to heal. Because our minds are so often thrown into a state of confusion by our anxieties and our hurts, we have lost the ability to connect with the wonderful things in life. It is as if there is a wall between us and the richness of the world outside us, and we have become numb

toward the healing things of the world because we cannot reach
them.

As you practice these two exercises, although you may not be in direct contact with the things you are asked to concentrate upon, you can find them by means of the images stored in consciousness by your five senses. You can call up these images when you want them to present themselves. With conscious breathing and the power of concentration, contact with these images will help you to discover that your ability to feel is still intact. After practicing these two exercises, you can go outside and with your *six* senses—eyes, ears, nose, tongue, body, and mind (that is, perception, not just the meditating mind)—continue making connections with all the good things around you. You will see that the outside world is brighter and more beautiful than before, because you have put an end to forgetfulness and have lit the lamp of mindfulness. You have begun again to be nourished by what is wonderful in life.

EXERCISE NINE

Looking Deeply

1. Aware of my body, I breathe in.   Aware of body
   Smiling to my body, I breathe out.   Smiling

2. Aware of the element earth in me,   Aware of earth
   I breathe in.
   Smiling to the element earth in me,   Smiling
   I breathe out.

3. Aware of the element water in me,   Aware of water
   I breathe in.
   Smiling to the element water in me,   Smiling
   I breathe out.

4. Aware of the element fire in me,   Aware of fire
   I breathe in.
   Smiling to the element fire in me,   Smiling
   I breathe out.

5. Aware of the element air in me,
   I breathe in.
   Smiling to the element air in me,
   I breathe out.

   Aware of air

   Smiling

6. Aware of the element space in me,
   I breathe in.
   Smiling to the element space in me,
   I breathe out.

   Aware of space

   Smiling

7. Aware of the element consciousness
   in me, I breathe in.
   Smiling to the element consciousness
   in me, I breathe out.

   Aware of
   consciousness
   Smiling

8. Recognizing the element earth
   everywhere, I breathe in.
   Smiling to the element earth
   everywhere, I breathe out.

   Recognizing earth

   Smiling

9. Seeing that the element earth
   contains water, fire, air, space, and
   consciousness, I breathe in.
   Seeing that earth is water, fire, air,
   space, and consciousness,
   I breathe out.

   Earth contains
   other elements

   Earth is the other
   elements

10. Recognizing the element water
    everywhere, I breathe in.
    Smiling to the element water
    everywhere I breathe out.

    Recognizing water

    Smiling

11. Seeing that the element water
contains earth, fire, air, space, and
consciousness, I breathe in.
Seeing that water is earth, fire, air,
space, and consciousness,
I breathe out.

Water contains
other elements

Water is the other
elements

12. Recognizing the element fire
everywhere, I breathe in.
Smiling to the element fire
everywhere, I breathe out.

Recognizing fire

Smiling

13. Seeing that the element fire contains
earth, water, air, space, and
consciousness, I breathe in.
Seeing that fire is earth, water, air,
space, and consciousness,
I breathe out.

Fire contains other
elements

Fire is the other
elements

14. Recognizing the element air
everywhere, I breathe in.
Smiling to the element air
everywhere, I breathe out.

Recognizing air

Smiling

15. Seeing that the element air contains
earth, water, fire, space, and
consciousness, I breathe in.
Seeing that air is earth, water, fire,
space, and consciousness,
I breathe out.

Air contains other
elements

Air is the other
elements

16. Recognizing the element space
everywhere, I breathe in.
Smiling to the element space
everywhere, I breathe out.

Recognizing space

Smiling

17. Seeing that the element space contains earth, water, fire, air, and consciousness, I breathe in.
Seeing that space is earth, water, fire, air, and consciousness, I breathe out.

Space contains other elements

Space is the other elements

18. Recognizing the element consciousness everywhere, I breathe in.
Smiling to the element consciousness everywhere, I breathe out.

Recognizing consciousness

Smiling

19. Seeing that the element consciousness contains earth, water, air, fire, and space, I breathe in.
Seeing that consciousness is earth, water, air, fire, and space, I breathe out.

Consciousness contains other elements
Consciousness is the other elements

This exercise leads us to the observation of the six elements which comprise both the human organism and the universe. The six elements are earth, water, fire, air, space, and consciousness. Earth stands for the solid aspect of things, water for the fluid, fire for warmth and heat, air for movement. Space and consciousness are nature and frame of the four first elements. When we breathe in, we see earth in our bodies. When we breathe out, we recognize and smile to that element earth. Earth is the mother who gives us birth and our mother is right inside us. We are one with our mother; we are one with the earth. Every moment earth is entering us. The vegetables we eat are also earth. As we meditate, we should see earth by means of concrete images. When we meditate on water in ourselves, we should see water in our blood, in our saliva, bile, and sweat, and we should smile to acknowledge water. Our bodies are approximately 70 percent water. We can also see air and space in our bodies. If we look deeply, we shall see that these elements all depend on each other. The air, for example, is nourished by the forest. The forest needs the air, which passes into tree sap in order to make chlorophyll. The vegetal world, including the vegetables we eat, requires the earth and the heat of the sun to grow. Neither space nor solid matter could exist without the other. The sutra teaches that form is also mind, and we see consciousness has penetrated every cell of our bodies. Consciousness upholds body and body upholds consciousness.

When we begin to meditate on earth, water, fire, air, space, and consciousness outside our bodies, we recognize that these six elements are everywhere in the universe. We gradually come to see that we and the universe are one. The universe is our basis, and we are the basis of the universe. The composition and the decomposition of a body does not add anything to or take away anything from the universe. The sun is just as necessary for our bodies as our hearts are. The forest is just as necessary for our bodies as are our lungs. Our bodies need the river as much as they need our blood. If we continue to meditate like this, we shall see that we can let go of the boundaries between "I" and "not I," and thus we can overcome the distinction between birth and death, being and nonbeing, and finally we can overcome fear. According to the principle of interdependent origination, the *one* comes about because of the *all* and the *all* is present in the *one*. Thus the earth element contains the water, heat, air, space, and consciousness elements. The earth element can be recognized as including the whole universe within itself. The Pali word *kasina* (Sanskrit

kṛtsna) is sometimes translated as "sign," meaning the sign that
we have realized the object of our meditation, but the original
meaning of the word is "wholeness," and when our meditation is
deep enough we see that each element contains all the others. Such
a practice is called *kṛtsnāyatanabhāvanā*, which means "training
in entering the whole." In *kṛtsnāyatanabhāvanā*, we can also
meditate on colors: blue, red, white, and yellow. These four colors
and the six elements make up ten trainings in entering the whole.
Colors are also present in the universe and in us, and every color
contains all the other colors and also contains the six elements
which are in us and in the whole universe.

EXERCISE TEN

Looking Deeply

1. Aware of the hair on my head,   Hair
   I breathe in.
   Seeing the impermanence of the hair   Impermanent
   on my head, I breathe out.

2. Aware of my eyes, I breathe in.   Eyes
   Seeing the impermanence of my   Impermanent
   eyes, I breathe out.

3. Aware of my ears, I breathe in.   Ears
   Seeing the impermanence of my   Impermanent
   ears, I breathe out.

4. Aware of my nose, I breathe in.   Nose
   Seeing the impermanence of my   Impermanent
   nose, I breathe out.

5. Aware of my tongue, I breathe in.   Tongue
   Seeing the impermanence of my   Impermanent
   tongue, I breathe out.

6. Aware of my heart, I breathe in.   Heart
   Seeing the impermanence of my   Impermanent
   heart, I breathe out.

7. Aware of my liver, I breathe in.   Liver
   Seeing the impermanence of my   Impermanent
   liver, I breathe out.

8. Aware of my lungs, I breathe in.   Lungs
   Seeing the impermanence of my   Impermanent
   lungs, I breathe out.

9. Aware of my intestines, I breathe in.   Intestines
   Seeing the impermanence of my   Impermanent
   intestines, I breathe out.

10. Aware of my kidneys, I breathe in.   Kidneys
    Seeing the impermanence of my   Impermanent
    kidneys, I breathe out.

11. Aware of my body, I breathe in.   Body
    Seeing the impermanence of my   Impermanent
    body, I breathe out.

12. Aware of the world, I breathe in.   The world
    Seeing the impermanence of the   Impermanent
    world, I breathe out.

13. Aware of my nation, I breathe in.   My nation
    Seeing the impermanence of my   Impermanent
    nation, I breathe out.

14. Aware of governments, I breathe in.   Governments
    Seeing the impermanence of   Impermanent
    governments, I breathe out.

This exercise helps us to acknowledge the impermanent nature of everything. The work of acknowledging everything in mindfulness leads us to a deeper view of what life is. It is very important to understand that impermanence is not a negative aspect of life. Impermanence is the very basis of life. If what exists were not impermanent, no life could continue. If a grain of corn were not impermanent, it could not become a corn plant. If a tiny child were not impermanent, she could not grow into an adult.

Life is impermanent, but that does not mean that it is not worth living. It is precisely because of its impermanence that we value life so dearly. Therefore we must know how to live each moment deeply and use it in a responsible way. If we are able to live the present moment completely, we will not feel regret later. We will know how to care for those who are close to us and how to bring them happiness. When we accept that all things are impermanent, we will not be incapacitated by suffering when things decay and die. We can remain peaceful and content in the face of change, prosperity and decline, success and failure.

Many people are always restless and in a hurry and do not know how to look after their bodies and minds. Night and day, bit by bit, they barter their health away in order to obtain material comforts. In the end, they destroy body and mind for the sake of these unimportant things. This exercise also can help us to look after our bodies and minds.

EXERCISE ELEVEN

Contemplation

1. Aware of my body alive and   Live body
   breathing, I breathe in.
   Smiling to my body alive and   Smiling
   breathing, I breathe out.

2. Seeing my dead body lying in bed,   Dead body
   I breathe in.
   Smiling to my dead body lying in   Smiling
   bed, I breathe out.

3. Seeing my dead body gray in color,   My gray body
   I breathe in.
   Smiling to my dead body gray in   Smiling
   color, I breathe out.

4. Seeing my dead body infested with   My infested body
   worms and flies, I breathe in.
   Smiling to my dead body infested   Smiling
   with worms and flies, I breathe out.

5. Seeing my dead body as a white skeleton, I breathe in.
Smiling to my dead body as a white skeleton, I breathe out.

My white skeleton

Smiling

6. Seeing my dead body as a number of fresh bones scattered here and there, I breathe in.
Smiling to my dead body as a number of fresh bones scattered here and there, I breathe out.

Scattered fresh bones

Smiling

7. Seeing my dead body as a number of dried bones, I breathe in.
Smiling to my dead body as a number of dried bones, I breathe out.

Dried bones

Smiling

8. Seeing my dead body being wrapped in a shroud, I breathe in.
Smiling to my dead body being wrapped in a shroud, I breathe out.

Wrapped in a shroud
Smiling

9. Seeing my dead body being placed in a coffin, I breathe in.
Smiling to my dead body being placed in a coffin I breathe out.

Placed in coffin

Smiling

10. Seeing my dead body being cremated, I breathe in.
Smiling to my dead body being cremated, I breathe out.

Cremated

Smiling

11. Seeing my mortal remains being mixed with the earth, I breathe in.
Smiling to my mortal remains being mixed with the earth, I breathe out.

Remains mixing with earth
Smiling

This exercise helps us become accustomed to the fact that sooner or later we all have to die. It is also a way of meditating on the impermanence of the body. It is traditionally known as the Nine Contemplations on the unclean *(navāśubha samjñā)*. If we can become familiar and comfortable with the idea that makes us afraid of death, we shall begin to transform that fear. We shall also begin to live our lives more deeply and with more care and awareness.

When we can envision and accept our own death, we are able to let go of many ambitions, worries, and sufferings. In short, we are able to let go of all the things which keep us so unnecessarily busy. We can begin to live in a way meaningful for ourselves and for other species.

The various stages of decomposition of the corpse which belong to the traditional Nine Contemplations can be replaced by simple images more appropriate to our own era, for example, a shroud, coffin, cremation furnace, vase of ashes, ashes becoming earth, or ashes scattered on the waves of a river or ocean.

EXERCISE TWELVE

Contemplation

1. Aware of my beloved alive and healthy, I breathe in.
   Smiling to my beloved alive and healthy, I breathe out.

   Beloved alive

   Smiling

2. Seeing the dead body of my beloved, I breathe in.
   Smiling to the dead body of my beloved, I breathe out.

   Seeing beloved dead
   Smiling

3. Seeing the dead body of my beloved gray in color, I breathe in.
   Smiling to the dead body of my beloved gray in color, I breathe out.

   Beloved's gray body
   Smiling

4. Seeing the dead body of my beloved infested with worms and flies, I breathe in.
   Smiling to the dead body of my beloved infested with worms and flies, I breathe out.

   Beloved's body infested

   Smiling

5. Seeing the dead body of my beloved as a white skeleton I breathe in. Smiling to the dead body of my beloved as a white skeleton I breathe out.

Beloved's skeleton

Smiling

6. Seeing my beloved's body as a number of fresh bones scattered here and there, I breathe in. Smiling to my beloved's body as a number of fresh bones scattered here and there, I breathe out.

Scattered fresh bones

Smiling

7. Seeing my beloved's body as a number of dried bones, I breathe in. Smiling to my beloved's body as a number of dried bones, I breathe out.

Dried bones

Smiling

8. Seeing my beloved's body being wrapped in a shroud, I breathe in. Smiling to my beloved's body being wrapped in a shroud, I breathe out.

Wrapped in a shroud
Smiling

9. Seeing my beloved's body being placed in a coffin, I breathe in. Smiling to my beloved's body being placed in a coffin, I breathe out.

Placed in coffin

Smiling

10. Seeing my beloved's body being cremated, I breathe in. Smiling to my beloved's body being cremated, I breathe out.

Cremated

Smiling

11. Seeing my beloved's remains being mixed with the earth, I breathe in. Smiling to my beloved's remains being mixed with the earth, I breathe out.

Remains mixing with earth
Smiling

This exercise helps us to accept that sooner or later those we love most will pass away. There is no escaping that fact. As in the preceding exercise, the images presented by the Nine Contemplations can be replaced by simpler ones.

When we can envision the death of one we love, we are able to let go of anger and reproachfulness toward that person. We learn to live in a sweeter way with those we love, to look after them and to make them happy. Our awareness of impermanence keeps thoughtless words and actions about those we love from invading our daily lives. We learn how to avoid hurting the ones most important to us and avoid sowing seeds of suffering in ourselves and in them.

EXERCISE THIRTEEN

Contemplation

1. Seeing the vigor and strength of the one who makes me suffer, I breathe in.
Smiling to the vigor and strength of the one who makes me suffer, I breathe out.

   The vigor of one who makes me suffer
   Smiling

2. Seeing the dead body of the one who makes me suffer, I breathe in.

   Smiling to the dead body of the one who makes me suffer, I breathe out.

   The dead body of one who makes me suffer
   Smiling

3. Seeing the dead body, gray in color, of the one who makes me suffer, I breathe in.
Smiling to the dead body, gray in color, of the one who makes me suffer, I breathe out.

   Gray corpse

   Smiling

4. Seeing the bloated dead body of the   Bloated corpse
   one who makes me suffer,
   I breathe in.
   Smiling to the bloated dead body of   Smiling
   the one who makes me suffer,
   I breathe out.

5. Seeing the festering dead body of the   Festering corpse
   one who makes me suffer,
   I breathe in.
   Smiling to the festering dead body of   Smiling
   the one who makes me suffer,
   I breathe out.

6. Seeing the dead body of the one who   Infested corpse
   makes me suffer infested with
   worms and flies, I breathe in.
   Smiling to the dead body of the one   Smiling
   who makes me suffer infested with
   worms and flies, I breathe out.

7. Seeing the white skeleton of the one   White skeleton
   who makes me suffer, I breathe in.
   Smiling to the white skeleton of the   Smiling
   one who makes me suffer,
   I breathe out.

8. Seeing the dead body of the one who   Scattered fresh
   makes me suffer as a number of   bones
   fresh bones scattered here and there,
   I breathe in.
   Smiling to the dead body of the one   Smiling
   who makes me suffer as a number of
   fresh bones scattered here and there,
   I breathe out.

9. Seeing the dead body of the one who makes me suffer as scattered dried bones, I breathe in.	Scattered dried bones	6 1
Smiling to the dead body of the one who makes me suffer as scattered dried bones, I breathe out.	Smiling	
10. Seeing the dead body of the one who makes me suffer as rotten bones turned to dust, I breathe in.	Rotten bones turned to dust	
Smiling to the dead body of the one who makes me suffer as rotten bones turned to dust, I breathe out.	Smiling	

This exercise is just like the two which precede it, but the object of the meditation is someone who makes us suffer so much that we are filled with hate and anger. We meditate in order to be able to see the frailty and the impermanence of those who hurt us. This meditation will dissolve our anger and foster love and compassion for someone we hate, and for ourselves too. Very often those with whom we get most angry are those we most love. Our anger is a function of that deep love, which can be released by the exercise.

EXERCISE FOURTEEN

Looking Deeply, Letting Go

1. Contemplating the attractive body of a woman, I breathe in.
Seeing the impermanent nature of that body, I breathe out.

   Attractive body

   Impermanent nature of body

2. Contemplating the attractive body of a man, I breathe in.
Seeing the impermanent nature of that body, I breathe out.

   Attractive body

   Impermanent nature of body

3. Contemplating the danger that my craving for sex can bring about, I breathe in.
Letting go of the craving, I breathe out.

   Danger from craving sex

   Letting go

4. Contemplating the suffering that my craving for sex can bring about, I breathe in.
Letting go of the craving, I breathe out.

   Suffering from craving sex

   Letting go

5. Contemplating the hardship that my
   craving for sex can bring about,
   I breathe in.
   Letting go of the craving,
   I breathe out.

Hardship from
craving sex

Letting go

6. Contemplating running after
   possessions, I breathe in.
   Seeing the impermanent nature of
   possessions, I breathe out.

Running after
possessions
Impermanent
nature of
possessions

7. Contemplating my desire for a car,
   I breathe in.
   Seeing the impermanent nature of a
   car, I breathe out.

Desire for a car

Impermanent
nature of car

8. Contemplating my desire for a
   house, I breathe in.
   Seeing the impermanent nature of a
   house, I breathe out.

Desire for a house

Impermanent
nature of house

9. Contemplating my desire for
   material security, I breathe in.
   Seeing the impermanent nature of
   material security, I breathe out.

Material security

Impermanent
nature of security

10. Contemplating the danger that my
    craving for wealth can bring about,
    I breathe in.
    Letting go of the craving,
    I breathe out.

Danger of craving
for wealth

Letting go

11. Contemplating the suffering that my craving for wealth can bring about, I breathe in.
Letting go of the craving, I breathe out.

Suffering from craving for wealth

Letting go

12. Contemplating the hardship that my craving for wealth can bring about, I breathe in.
Letting go of the craving, I breathe out.

Hardship from craving for wealth

Letting go

13. Contemplating the pursuit of fame, I breathe in.
Seeing the impermanent nature of that fame, I breathe out.

Pursuit of fame

Impermanent nature of fame

14. Contemplating the danger that my craving for fame can bring about, I breathe in.
Letting go of the craving, I breathe out.

Danger of craving for fame

Letting go

15. Contemplating the suffering that my craving for fame can bring about, I breathe in.
Letting go of the craving, I breathe out.

Suffering from craving for fame

Letting go

16. Contemplating the hardship that my craving for fame can bring about, I breathe in.
Letting go of the craving, I breathe out.

Hardship from craving for fame

Letting go

17. Contemplating my greed for clothes and food, I breathe in.	Greediness
Seeing the impermanent nature of clothes and food, I breathe out.	Impermanent nature of clothes and food
18. Contemplating the danger that my greed for clothes and food can bring about, I breathe in.	Danger from greediness
Letting go of the greed, I breathe out.	Letting go
19. Contemplating the suffering that my greed for clothes and food can bring about, I breathe in.	Suffering from greediness
Letting go of the greed, I breathe out.	Letting go
20. Contemplating the hardship that my greed for clothes and food can bring about, I breathe in.	Hardship from greediness
Letting go of the greed, I breathe out.	Letting go
21. Contemplating an indolent life, I breathe in.	Indolent life
Seeing the danger of an indolent life, I breathe out.	Danger
22. Contemplating letting go, I breathe in.	Letting go
Contemplating letting go, I breathe out.	Letting go

This exercise helps us to see the impermanence as well as the dangers, complications, and hardships of our endless pursuit of material and sensual pleasure—whether that pleasure takes the form of a beautiful man or woman, riches and possessions, fame, or other objects of desire. We suffer countless agonies large and small in order to enjoy these sensual pleasures. We could waste our whole lives chasing after them without there being any guarantee that we would attain them. Even if we did attain them, we would discover that they are not only short-lived but also dangerous to the well-being of the body and mind.

Real happiness cannot exist when we are not totally free. Burdened by so many ambitions, we are not able to be free. We are always grasping at something; there are so many things we want to do at the same time, and that is why we do not have the time to live. We think that the burdens we carry are necessary for our happiness, that if they are taken from us we will suffer. However, if we look more closely, we shall see that the things at which we grasp, the things that keep us constantly busy, are in fact obstacles to our being happy. The practice of this meditation exercise should be followed with the practice of exercises which help us to let go, like the following one. In letting go, we learn that true happiness can only come by way of freedom, an awakened life, and the practice of love and compassion.

EXERCISE FIFTEEN

Looking Deeply, Healing

1. Knowing I will get old, I breathe in.　　Getting old
   Knowing I can't escape old age,　　　　No escape
   I breathe out.

2. Knowing I will get sick, I breathe in.　Getting sick
   Knowing I can't escape sickness,　　　No escape
   I breathe out.

3. Knowing I will die, I breathe in.　　　Dying
   Knowing I can't escape death,　　　　No escape
   I breathe out.

4. Knowing that one day I will have to　　Abandoning what
   abandon all that I cherish today,　　　I cherish
   I breathe in.
   Knowing I can't escape having to　　　No escape
   abandon all that I cherish today,
   I breathe out.

5. Knowing that my actions are my
   only belongings, I breathe in.
   Knowing that I cannot escape the
   consequences of my actions,
   I breathe out.

   Actions true
   belongings
   No escape from
   consequences

6. Determined to live my days deeply
   in mindfulness, I breathe in.
   Seeing the joy and the benefit of
   living mindfully, I breathe out.

   Living mindfully

   Seeing joy

7. Vowing to offer joy each day to my
   beloved, I breathe in.
   Vowing to ease the pain of my
   beloved, I breathe out.

   Offering joy

   Easing pain

This exercise helps us to come face to face with anxieties and fears that lie deep in our subconscious, and to transform the latent tendencies called *anuśaya* by Buddhists. In principle, we all know very well that we cannot avoid growing old, falling sick, dying, and being separated from those we love, but we do not want to give our attention to these things. We do not want to be in touch with the anxiety and the fear but prefer to let them sleep deep in our minds. That is why they are called latent tendencies (the word *anuśaya* literally means "lying asleep along with"). But although they are lying asleep in our hearts, they still follow us and secretly influence our whole way of thinking, speaking, and acting. When we hear people speaking about, or are ourselves witness to, old age, sickness, death, and separations from loved ones, the latent tendencies in us are watered and become more deeply rooted—along with our other sorrows, longings, hatreds, and angers. Because we are

not able to resolve the *anuśaya,* we repress them, and they grow
stagnant and cause sickness whose symptoms can be recognized in
everything we do. We must learn a different way to treat the
anusaya. The Buddha himself taught this exercise and advised his
followers to practice it every day. Buddha taught that rather than
repressing our fears and anxieties, we should invite them into
consciousness, recognize them, welcome them. When we begin to
practice conscious breathing, mindfulness is lit up within us. In
that gentle light, if we simply acknowledge the presence of our
fears and smile to them as we would smile to an old friend, quite
naturally they will lose some of their energy. When once again
they return to our subconscious, they will be that much weaker.
If we practice every day, they will continue to grow weaker. The
circulation of feelings in our consciousness under the light of
mindfulness will prevent their stagnation, we will see into their
essence, and there will be no more manifestations of the former
mental and physical sicknesses. The latent tendencies will have
been transformed.

This exercise also helps us to live the present moment in a
joyous, calm, and awakened way. Right in this moment, we will
come to understand, we are able to bring joy to those in our
company.

EXERCISE SIXTEEN

Looking Deeply, Healing

1. Aware of my body, I breathe in.
   Smiling to my body, I breathe out.

   Aware of body
   Smiling

2. Experiencing the pain in my body,
   I breathe in.
   Smiling to the pain in my body,
   I breathe out.

   Experiencing
   physical pain
   Smiling

3. Recognizing that this is a physical
   pain, I breathe in.
   Knowing that this is no more than a
   physical pain, I breathe out.

   Recognizing pain
   as physical
   Only physical pain

4. Aware of the contents of my mind,
   I breathe in.
   Smiling to the contents of my mind,
   I breathe out.

   Aware of mind

   Smiling

5. Experiencing the pain in my mind,
I breathe in.
Smiling to the pain in my mind,
I breathe out.

Experiencing
mind's pain
Smiling

6. Experiencing the pain of fear in me,
I breathe in.
Smiling to the pain of fear in me,
I breathe out.

Experiencing fear

Smiling

7. Experiencing the feeling of insecurity
in me, I breathe in.
Smiling to the feeling of insecurity,
I breathe out.

Experiencing
insecurity
Smiling

8. Experiencing the feeling of sadness
in me, I breathe in.
Smiling to the feeling of sadness in
me, I breathe out.

Experiencing
sadness
Smiling

9. Experiencing the feeling of anger in
me, I breathe in.
Smiling to the feeling of anger in
me, I breathe out.

Experiencing anger

Smiling

10. Experiencing the feeling of jealousy
in me, I breathe in.
Smiling to the feeling of jealousy in
me, I breathe out.

Experiencing
jealousy
Smiling

11. Experiencing the feeling of
attachment in me, I breathe in.
Smiling to the feeling of attachment
in me, I breathe out.

Experiencing
attachment
Smiling

12. Experiencing the feeling of joy in me, I breathe in.	Experiencing joy
Smiling to the feeling of joy in me, I breathe out.	Smiling
13. Experiencing the joy of liberty in me, I breathe in.	Joy of liberty
Smiling to the joy of liberty in me, I breathe out.	Smiling
14. Experiencing the joy of release in me, I breathe in.	Joy of release
Smiling to the joy of release in me, I breathe out.	Smiling
15. Experiencing the joy of abandoning in me, I breathe in.	Joy of abandoning
Smiling to the joy of abandoning in me, I breathe out.	Smiling
16. Experiencing the neutral feeling in me, I breathe in.	Neutral feeling
Smiling to the neutral feeling in me, I breathe out.	Smiling

This exercise is to help us be in touch with all the feelings that arise in our minds. The feelings are either pleasant, unpleasant, or neutral. We must learn to recognize, acknowledge, and welcome each one, and after that to look into its impermanence. A feeling or an emotion arises, persists, and then disappears. Mindfulness enables us to be calm throughout the appearance and disappearance of feelings. Buddha taught us not to be attached to feelings but also not to push them away. To acknowledge feelings with an even mind is the very best way; while we are acknowledging them in mindfulness, slowly, slowly we come to a deep realization of their nature. It is that insight which will enable us to be free and at ease as we face each feeling.

Feelings of fear, anxiety, anger, jealousy, and attachment are often unpleasant or painful. The steady practice of mindfulness will help us to acknowledge the painful feeling whenever it appears. In this way, we can avoid being drowned by waves of feelings, however powerful they may be. Sitting easily, we should bring our attention to the part of the abdomen just below the navel. From the rising and falling of the abdomen, we should become aware of our in-breathing and out-breathing for the duration of ten or fifteen minutes. In that time, peace of mind will be gradually restored, and we shall not be blown away by gales of emotion. As we continue to acknowledge and look deeply, we shall see the essence of each feeling and emotion as it arises.

We should acknowledge and look deeply at pleasant feelings as well as painful ones, for states of mind born from freedom, release, and letting go are healthy and nourishing. Acknowledged in mindfulness, these states of mind are able to develop and last. Mindful breathing is the wholesome food for these feelings, which are so necessary in our lives.

A neutral feeling is neither pleasant nor painful. But when such feelings are recognized in mindfulness, they usually become pleasant feelings. This is one of the benefits of insight meditation. When you have a toothache the feeling is very unpleasant, and when you do not have a toothache you usually have a neutral feeling. However, if you can be mindful of the nontoothache, the nontoothache will become a feeling of peace and joy. Mindfulness gives rise to and nourishes happiness.

EXERCISE SEVENTEEN

Looking Deeply, Healing

1. Aware of my body, I breathe in.
   Smiling to my body, I breathe out.

   Aware of body
   Smiling

2. Looking at the roots of the pain in
   my body, I breathe in.
   Smiling to the roots of the pain in
   my body, I breathe out.

   Roots of physical
   pain
   Smiling

3. Aware of the contents of my mind,
   I breathe in.
   Smiling to the contents of my mind,
   I breathe out.

   Aware of mind

   Smiling

4. Looking at the roots of the pain in
   my mind, I breathe in.
   Smiling to the roots of the pain in
   my mind, I breathe out.

   Roots of mind's
   pain
   Smiling

5. Looking at the roots of the pain of fear, I breathe in.
Smiling to the roots of the pain of fear, I breathe out.

Roots of fear

Smiling

6. Looking at the roots of the feeling of insecurity, I breathe in.
Smiling to the roots of the feeling of insecurity, I breathe out.

Roots of insecurity

Smiling

7. Looking at the roots of the feeling of sadness, I breathe in.
Smiling to the roots of the feeling of sadness, I breathe out.

Roots of sadness

Smiling

8. Looking at the roots of the feeling of anger, I breathe in.
Smiling to the roots of the feeling of anger, I breathe out.

Roots of anger

Smiling

9. Looking at the roots of the feeling of jealousy, I breathe in.
Smiling to the roots of the feeling of jealousy, I breathe out.

Roots of jealousy

Smiling

10. Looking at the roots of the feeling of attachment, I breathe in.
Smiling to the roots of the feeling of attachment, I breathe out.

Roots of attachment

Smiling

11. Looking at the roots of the feeling of being caught, I breathe in.
Smiling to the roots of the feeling of being caught, I breathe out.

Roots of being caught

Smiling

12. Looking at the roots of the feeling of joy, I breathe in.

    Roots of joy

    Smiling to the roots of the feeling of joy, I breathe out.

    Smiling

13. Looking at the roots of the joy of liberty, I breathe in.

    Roots of joy of liberty

    Smiling to the roots of the joy of liberty, I breathe out.

    Smiling

14. Looking at the roots of the joy of release, I breathe in.

    Roots of joy of release

    Smiling to the roots of the joy of release, I breathe out.

    Smiling

15. Looking at the roots of the joy of abandoning, I breathe in.

    Roots of joy of abandoning

    Smiling to the roots of the joy of abandoning, I breathe out.

    Smiling

16. Looking at the roots of the neutral feeling, I breathe in.

    Roots of neutral feeling

    Smiling to the roots of the neutral feeling, I breathe out.

    Smiling

To oppose, brush aside, or deny pain in our body or mind only makes that feeling more intense. In the preceding exercises, we have practiced acknowledging and accepting painful feelings. Our painful feelings are not other than ourselves, or to put it more precisely, they are a part of us. To deny them is to deny our very selves. The moment we accept these feelings, we begin to feel more peaceful, and the pain begins to lose some of its intensity. To smile to our pain is the wisest, the most intelligent, the most beautiful thing we can do. There is no better way.

Every time we acknowledge a feeling of pain and make its

acquaintance, we come in closer contact with ourselves. Bit by bit we look deeply into the substance and the roots of that pain. Fear, insecurity, anger, sadness, jealousy, and attachment form blocks of feelings and thoughts within us (Sanskrit *samyojana*, "internal formation"), and we need time and opportunity to acknowledge them and to look into them. The mindfulness of breathing does the work of making painful feelings bearable. Mindfulness recognizes the presence of the feelings, acknowledges them, soothes them, and enables the work of observation to continue until the substance of the block is seen. Mindfulness is the only way to transform it. All the seeds of pain are present within us, and if we live in forgetfulness, the seeds of pain will be watered every day. They will grow strong, and the internal blocks will become more solid. Conscious breathing transforms internal formations of painful feelings.

Internal formations can also be seen as "fetters" or "knots" of suffering deep in our consciousness. The knots are created when we react emotionally to what others say and do, and also when we repeatedly suppress our awareness of both pleasant and unpleasant feelings and thoughts. The fetters which bind us can be identified as any painful feeling or addictive pleasant feeling, such as anger, hatred, pride, doubt, sorrow, or attachment. They are forged by confusion and a lack of understanding, by our misperceptions regarding our selves and our reality. By practicing mindfulness, we are able to recognize and transform unpleasant feelings and emotions when they first arise, so they do not become fetters. When we do not let ourselves react to the words and actions of others, when we are able to keep our minds calm and peaceful, the fetters of internal formations cannot be made, and we will experience greater happiness and joy. Our families, friends, and associates will also benefit from our greater understanding and love.

In our consciousness there are also the seeds of happiness, such as a loving heart, the ability to let go, joy, calm, and freedom. But these seeds need water every day or they will never thrive. When we are able to nourish these seeds with mindfulness, they will burst into bloom and offer us the flowers and fruits of happiness. This is the object of the latter part of the exercise. This exercise does not need to be practiced all at one time. It can be divided into several shorter exercises to be practiced over a long period of time, say, three to six months.

EXERCISE EIGHTEEN

EXERCISE EIGHTEEN

Looking Deeply, Healing

1. Seeing myself as a five-year-old
child, I breathe in.
Smiling to the five-year-old child,
I breathe out.

   Myself five years
old
Smiling

2. Seeing the five-year-old as fragile
and vulnerable, I breathe in.
Smiling with love to the
five-year-old in me, I breathe out.

   Five-year-old
fragile
Smiling with love

3. Seeing my father as a five-year-old
boy, I breathe in.
Smiling to my father as a
five-year-old boy, I breathe out.

   Father five years
old
Smiling

4. Seeing my five-year-old father as
fragile and vulnerable, I breathe in.
Smiling with love and understanding
to my father as a five-year-old boy,
I breathe out.

   Father fragile and
vulnerable
Smiling with love
and understanding

5. Seeing my mother as a five-year-old girl, I breathe in.
Smiling to my mother as a five-year-old girl, I breathe out.

Mother five years old
Smiling

6. Seeing my five-year-old mother as fragile and vulnerable, I breathe in.
Smiling with love and understanding to my mother as a five-year-old girl, I breathe out.

Mother fragile and vulnerable
Smiling with love and understanding

7. Seeing my father suffering as a child, I breathe in.
Seeing my mother suffering as a child, I breathe out.

Father suffering as a child
Mother suffering as a child

8. Seeing my father in me, I breathe in.
Smiling to my father in me, I breathe out.

Father in me
Smiling

9. Seeing my mother in me, I breathe in.
Smiling to my mother in me, I breathe out.

Mother in me

Smiling

10. Understanding the difficulties that my father in me has, I breathe in.
Determined to work for the release of both my father and me, I breathe out.

Difficulties of father in me
Releasing father and me

11. Understanding the difficulties that my mother in me has, I breathe in.
Determined to work for the release of both my mother and me, I breathe out.

Difficulties of mother in me
Releasing mother and me

This exercise has helped many young people re-establish happy and stable relations with their parents. At the same time, it has helped them transform accumulated hatred and resentment which began gathering in them at a very young age.

There are people who cannot even think about their mothers and fathers without feelings of hatred and sorrow. There are always seeds of love in the hearts of parents and children, but because we do not know how to water those seeds, and especially because we do not know how to resolve resentments when they are newly sown, both generations often find it extremely difficult to accept each other.

For the first step of the exercise, the practitioner observes herself as a five-year-old child. At that age we are so easily hurt. An overly severe glance or a threatening or reproachful word wounds us deeply and makes us feel very ashamed. When father makes mother suffer or mother makes father suffer, a seed of suffering is also sown and watered in the heart of the child. If this happens repeatedly, the child will grow up with many seeds of suffering in her heart and will blame her father or her mother throughout her life. When we see ourselves as vulnerable children, we learn to feel compassion for ourselves, and that compassion will have a deep impact upon us. We must smile at that child of five years with the smile of compassion.

In the next stage of the meditation, the practitioner visualizes his mother or his father as a five-year-old child. Usually we think of our fathers as strict and severe, hard-to-please adults who only know how to resolve a problem by using their authority. But we also know that before a father was an adult, he once was a little boy, just as vulnerable, just as fragile as we ourselves were. We can see that that little boy cringed, fell silent, and did not dare open his mouth to speak whenever his own father fell into a rage. We see that small boy may also have been the victim of the hot temper, scowling, and roughness of a father. It is often helpful to seek out an old family photograph album to find out what our mothers or fathers looked like when they were young children. In our sitting meditation, we can welcome the children who were our mothers and fathers and smile to them as we would smile to dear friends. We see their fragility and their vulnerability and a feeling of pity for them is born in us. When this feeling of pity wells up in our hearts, we know that our meditation is beginning to bear fruit. When we truly see and understand someone's suffering, it is impossible not to accept and love them. The accumulated resentment toward our parents will gradually be transformed as we practice this exercise. As we grow in understanding, so we grow in acceptance. We shall be able to use this understanding and love to go to our parents and to help them transform too. We know that this is possible because our understanding and our feelings of compassion have helped us transform ourselves and we have already become easier, sweeter, calmer, and more tolerant people. Tolerance and calm are two signs of authentic love.

EXERCISE NINETEEN

Looking Deeply

1. Aware of my in-breath, I breathe in.
   Seeing my in-breath no longer there,
   I breathe out.

   Aware of in-breath
   In-breath no
   longer there

2. Aware of the birth of my in-breath,
   I breathe in.
   Aware of the death of my in-breath,
   I breathe out.

   Birth of in-breath

   Death of in-breath

3. Seeing my in-breath born from
   conditions, I breathe in.
   Seeing my in-breath die from
   conditions, I breathe out.

   Birth of in-breath
   conditional
   Death of in-breath
   conditional

4. Seeing my in-breath comes from
   nowhere, I breathe in.
   Seeing my in-breath goes nowhere,
   I breathe out.

   Breath from
   nowhere
   Breath going
   nowhere

5. Seeing my in-breath without birth
   and death, I breathe in.
   Seeing my in-breath free from birth
   and death, I breathe out.

   Breath without
   birth-death
   Free from
   birth-death

6. Aware of my eyes, I breathe in.
   Seeing my eyes born from
   conditions, I breathe out.

   Aware of eyes
   Eyes conditional

7. Seeing my eyes come from nowhere,
   I breathe in.
   Seeing my eyes go nowhere,
   I breathe out.

   Eyes from nowhere

   Eyes going
   nowhere

8. Seeing my eyes have no birth and
   death, I breathe in.
   Seeing my eyes free from birth and
   death, I breathe out.

   Eyes without
   birth-death
   Eyes free from
   birth-death

9. Aware of my body, I breathe in.
   Seeing my body born from
   conditions, I breathe out.

   Aware of body
   Body conditional

10. Seeing my body comes from
    nowhere, I breathe in.
    Seeing my body goes nowhere,
    I breathe out.

    Body from
    nowhere
    Body going
    nowhere

11. Seeing my body has no birth and
    death, I breathe in.
    Seeing my body free from birth and
    death, I breathe out.

    Body without
    birth-death
    Free from
    birth-death

12. Aware of my consciousness,
    I breathe in.
    Seeing my consciousness born from
    conditions, I breathe out.

    Aware of
    consciousness
    Consciousness
    conditional

13. Seeing my consciousness comes from
nowhere, I breathe in.
Seeing my consciousness goes
nowhere, I breathe out.

Consciousness
from nowhere
Consciousness
goes nowhere

14. Seeing my consciousness has no
birth and death, I breathe in.
Seeing my consciousness free from
birth and death, I breathe out.

Consciousness
without birth-death
Free from
birth-death

This exercise helps us to realize that nothing comes and nothing goes, nothing is born and nothing dies. This is one of the most wonderful practices of meditation in Buddhism.

To start with, we try to see the presence of each breath, in order to be aware of the birth and the death of that breath. As we begin to breathe in we see the in-breath being born, and as we begin to breathe out we see the in-breath has died. Birth and death are two marks of a breath. As we continue the meditation, we see that the occurrence of our in-breath is dependent on various causes and conditions: the lungs, respiratory muscles, the body, the atmosphere, the nose, the bronchial tubes, being alive, and so on. As we breathe out we see that the ending of the in-breath is also due to causes and conditions, and we become physically aware of those conditions. For example, the lungs are now full of air and are not able or do not want to breathe in anymore. As we meditate, we see that when the causes and conditions are right the breath is born, and when the right causes and conditions are not present it dies. We see that our breath at its birth does not come from anywhere and at its death does not go anywhere. There is no place in space where it comes from when it is born and there is no place in space it goes to when it dies. Then we see the not-coming, not-going marks of the breath. Looking more deeply, we see that a breath is not born and does not die but only manifests itself or lies hidden. Being born usually means that something comes into existence that did not exist before. Dying usually means something that has existed ceases to exist. But our breath is not like that. We cannot say that it did not exist before, only that because the conditions are sufficient and right it can manifest itself. If one of those conditions is absent, the breath goes into hiding. It is with regard to our perception that we talk about manifesting and failing to manifest. Manifest does not mean that something exists and not manifest does not mean that something fails to exist. Marks like birth and death, being and nonbeing are assigned to the breath by our perception. The real marks of the breath are no-birth, no-death, no-existence, no-nonexistence. The realization of this arises with our willingness to persevere in looking deeply into causes and conditions.

When we meditate on our eyes, we see that our eyes too are manifested dependent on conditions and go into hiding dependent on conditions. Our eyes do not come from anywhere and do not go away to any place. Eyes manifesting does not mean that eyes exist, and eyes going into hiding does not mean that eyes fail to exist. We cannot say that our eyes are born because they manifest, and we cannot say that they die because they fail to manifest. The same is true of our bodies and our consciousness. The true nature of the five aggregates (body, feelings, perceptions, mental forma- tions, and consciousness) is no-birth, no-death, no-existence and no-nonexistence. Birth and death are both illusory. To be or not to be, that is not the question.

EXERCISE TWENTY

Looking Deeply

1. Seeing my eyes, I breathe in.
   Smiling to my eyes, I breathe out.

   Seeing my eyes
   Smiling

2. Seeing my eyes are brought about
   by the coming together of the four
   elements, I breathe in.
   Seeing my eyes cease to be with the
   dissolution of the four elements,
   I breathe out.

   Eyes made of four
   elements

   Elements
   dissolved, eyes
   cease to be

3. Seeing my eyes containing the
   sunshine, I breathe in.
   Seeing my eyes containing the cloud,
   I breathe out.

   Eyes contain
   sunshine
   Eyes contain clouds

4. Seeing my eyes containing the earth,
   I breathe in.
   Seeing my eyes containing the air,
   I breathe out.

   Eyes contain earth

   Eyes contain air

5. Seeing my eyes containing the whole cosmos, I breathe in.	Eyes contain cosmos
Seeing my eyes present in everything in the cosmos, I breathe out.	Eyes in everything
6. Seeing my eyes as interbeing elements, I breathe in.	Eyes interare
Seeing all in the cosmos as interbeing elements, I breathe out.	All in cosmos interis
7. Seeing the all in the one, I breathe in.	All in one
Seeing the one in the many, I breathe out.	One in all things
8. Seeing the one as basic to the all, I breathe in.	One as basis of all
Seeing all things as basic to the one, I breathe out.	All things as basis of one
9. Seeing the birthless nature of my eyes, I breathe in.	Eyes birthless
Seeing the deathless nature of my eyes, I breathe out.	Eyes deathless

This exercise is a continuation of exercise nineteen. Its purpose is to help us look deeply at the conditional arising of all things, as well as the interdependence and interpenetration of all that exists. All that exists is impermanent. If something is born it must die, and this birth and death is taking place in every instant (Sanskrit *kṣaṇa*, the shortest instant of time). We realize this each time we meditate on impermanence. However, if we look deeper still, we shall see that impermanence means all things arise in dependence on each other. All that exists comes to be, endures, and

disappears because of certain causes and conditions: *This is because*
that is. This is not because that is not. This is born because that is born. This ceases to be because that ceases to be. This is the principle of dependent arising which is taught in the Madhyama and Samyukta Āgamas. When we look deeper still, we see that because everything arises in dependence on something else, there is no such thing as a separately existing self-nature. We come to see that all things are in essence empty: *This contains that and that contains this*—the principle of interpenetration. *This is that and that is this*—the principle of interbeing. Time contains time and time contains space. Space contains space and space contains time. Space is itself time. Space and time cannot exist separately from each other. One *kṣaṇa* (point instant) contains infinite time, and the smallest particle contains limitless space. This is the principle of all is one and one is all. When we understand that principle, the phenomena we have spoken of as birth, death, being, and nonbeing are seen to be illusions. We are able to see into the birthless and deathless nature of reality, which is sometimes called *dharmadhātu* (the true nature of the phenomenal world), *tathata* (suchness), *nirvana* (extinction of illusion and sorrow), and perfected truth. Concepts of birth, death, one, many, coming, going, purity, defilement, increasing, decreasing thus cannot be used to describe reality. Only when we realize the birthless and deathless nature of reality will we overcome the fears and sorrows that fetter us. That realization is a liberation.

Exercises nineteen and twenty need to be practiced diligently; not just during times of sitting meditation but throughout our daily lives.

EXERCISE TWENTY-ONE

Looking Deeply

1. Aware of a wave on the ocean,   Wave on the ocean
   I breathe in.
   Smiling to the wave on the ocean,   Smiling
   I breathe out.

2. Aware of the water in the wave,   Water in wave
   I breathe in.
   Smiling to the water in the wave,   Smiling
   I breathe out.

3. Seeing the birth of a wave,   Birth of a wave
   I breathe in.
   Smiling to the birth of the wave,   Smiling
   I breathe out.

4. Seeing the death of a wave,   Death of a wave
   I breathe in.
   Smiling to the death of the wave,   Smiling
   I breathe out.

5. Seeing the birthless nature of the water in the wave, I breathe in. Smiling to the birthless nature of the water in the wave, I breathe out.

6. Seeing the deathless nature of the water in the wave, I breathe in. Smiling to the deathless nature of the water in the wave, I breathe out.

Deathless water in wave
Smiling

7. Seeing the birth of my body, I breathe in. Smiling to the birth of my body, I breathe out.

Birth of my body

Smiling

8. Seeing the death of my body, I breathe in. Smiling to the death of my body, I breathe out.

Death of my body

Smiling

9. Seeing the birthless nature of my body, I breathe in. Smiling to the birthless nature of my body, I breathe out.

Body birthless

Smiling

10. Seeing the deathless nature of my body, I breathe in. Smiling to the deathless nature of my body, I breathe out.

Body deathless

Smiling

11. Seeing the birthless nature of my consciousness, I breathe in. Smiling to the birthless nature of my consciousness, I breathe out.

Consciousness birthless
Smiling

12. Seeing the deathless nature of my   Consciousness
consciousness, I breathe in.   deathless
Smiling to the deathless nature of   Smiling
my consciousness, I breathe out.

This exercise goes along with the two preceding exercises (exercises nineteen and twenty), and its aim is to help us look deeply into the true nature of all things. The phenomenal world seems to be marked by oppositions: birth/death, coming/going, being/nonbeing, one/many, defilement/purity, and so on. Mindful meditation enables us to see beyond such notions as these. The three seals of Buddhist teaching are impermanence, selflessness, and nirvana. Because things are impermanent and without a self, we say that they are born and die, come and go, still exist or no longer exist, are one or many, are defiled or pure. But Buddhism does more than reveal the phenomenal aspect of reality; it puts us in touch with the true nature (Sanskrit *svabhāva*) of phenomena. That true nature is nirvana. Nirvana cannot be described by means of either/or concepts. Nirvana means the putting to rest of all oppositional terms and notions. It also means the putting to rest of afflictions like desire, hatred, and ignorance that are born from these notions.

In the *Udāna* (Words of Uplift), Buddha speaks of nirvana in the following way (let us be very careful not to be caught in words and ideas, because the Buddha has also taught that it is impossible to say anything about the true nature of nirvana): "Monks, there is a place which is not the place of earth, water, air, or fire, limitless space or limitless consciousness, limitless nonmateriality, perceptions or no perceptions, this world or that world. I do not talk about this place as coming and going or not coming and not going, as being born and dying. This place does not come into existence or pass away and it does not need to rely on something else. It is the ending of all sorrow. It is nirvana." And again in the *Udāna:* "Monks, there is something which is not born, which is not conditional, which does not become, is not made, is not a composite. Supposing that this nonborn, nonconditional, not-become, not made, not compounded is not there, how could there be a place for the born, the conditional, the becoming, the made, the compounded to return to?"

Suppose that while we are listening to the Buddha speaking like this, we are caught in the words, "There is a place which . . . This place." Then there will be no way we shall be able to understand, because the reality of nirvana goes beyond all ideas of is or is not, one or many, place and no place, this and that. This exercise uses the image of a wave and the water as a metaphor for nirvana. The wave is birth and death; the water is nirvana. The wave is born and dies, rises and falls, is high and is low, comes to be and passes away, is many and is one. This is not true of the water in the wave. We should remember that this is only a metaphor. In our common perception water still belongs to the phenomenal world, like clouds, vapor, ice, and snow. Because we are able to look deeply at the phenomenal world, we are able to discover its birthless and death-less nature and to enter the world of suchness. In Buddhist studies, we talk about the process of going from the mark (*lakṣaṇa*) to the nature (*svabhāva*), from the sign to the essence.

A bodhisattva is able to see the nature of all that is and therefore is no longer afraid and no longer desires to hold on. Thus she can ride on the waves of birth and death with complete equanimity.

EXERCISE TWENTY-TWO

Looking Deeply

1. Aware of my body, I breathe in.   Aware of body
   Smiling to my body, I breathe out.   Smiling

2. Aware that this body is not me,   Body not me
   I breathe in.
   Aware that no self owns this body,   No self owns body
   I breathe out.

3. Aware of a feeling present now,   Aware of feeling
   I breathe in.
   Smiling to this feeling, I breathe out.   Smiling

4. Aware that this feeling is not me,   Feeling not me
   I breathe in.
   Aware that no self owns this feeling,   No self owns
   I breathe out.   feeling

5. Aware of a perception present now,   Aware of
   I breathe in.   perception
   Smiling to this perception,   Smiling
   I breathe out.

6. Aware that this perception is not me,
I breathe in.
Aware that no self owns this
perception, I breathe out.

Perception not me 95

No self owns
perception

7. Aware of a mental formation present
now, I breathe in.
Smiling to this mental formation,
I breathe out.

Aware of mental
formation
Smiling

8. Aware that this mental formation is
not me, I breathe in.
Aware that no self owns this mental
formation, I breathe out.

Mental formation
not me
No self owns
mental formation

9. Aware of consciousness being
present, I breathe in.
Smiling to this consciousness,
I breathe out.

Aware of
consciousness
Smiling

10. Aware that this consciousness is not
me, I breathe in.
Aware that no self owns this
consciousness, I breathe out.

Consciousness not
me
No self owns
consciousness

11. Knowing I am not limited by this
body, I breathe in.
Knowing this body is not limited by
my lifespan, I breathe out.

I not limited

Body not limited

12. Knowing that this body as five
aggregates is birthless and deathless,
I breathe in.
Knowing that I am also birthless and
deathless, I breathe out.

Body birthless,
deathless

I birthless,
deathless

13. Smiling to the birthlessness and
    deathlessness of this body,
    I breathe in.
    Smiling to the birthlessness and
    deathlessness of this self,
    I breathe out.

Smiling to
birthless, deathless
body
Smiling to
birthless, deathless
self

This exercise helps us to look deeply at the nature of selflessness. The body and the other bases of perception (eyes, ears, nose, tongue, and mind) are not the self. Nor do they belong to a self that lies outside them. The five aggregates are the body, the feelings, the perceptions, mental formations, and consciousness. These five aggregates are not the self, and they are also not the property of a self that exists apart from them. Self is often defined as a changeless entity existing independently from so-called nonself entities. Buddhism teaches that there is no such self, because in reality there is nothing changeless which can exist independently of all else. What then, is, the meaning of the words "I" and "self" in exercise twenty-two, and what do they refer to? Obviously "I" here refers to the person who is meditating, who is a compound of the five aggregates. The five aggregates are themselves a river of constantly transforming phenomena which are not separate entities. If we understand that, then there is nothing wrong with the use of the word "I." If our minds are open to the fact that self is made of nonself elements, we can use the expression "self" without fear—like Buddha when he asked Ananda: "Do *you* wish to come to Vulture peak with *me?*"

The wrong views of self can be enumerated as follows:

1. The body is the self *(Satkāyadṛṣṭi)*.
2. The body is not the self but it belongs to the self.

3. The body is in the self and the self is in the body.
4. The body is not the self but it is also not something independent of the self.
5. The world is the self, the self is the world.

It is important to remember that we meditate on no-self in order to uproot the idea of a permanent and changeless self-substance, not to establish a theory of nihilism. Eternalism and nihilism are both wrong views, traps which the Buddha taught his disciples to avoid. The view of permanence (Pali *sassata-diṭṭhi*) and the view that nothing is (Pali *uccheda diṭṭhi*) are the basis of all wrong thinking. If we are able to go beyond these two extremes, we can freely and as we please use the word "I," just as the Buddha used "This body is not me" or "I am not this body." To identify self with the world is also a confused notion if it means we are caught in "eternalist" or nihilistic thinking: "I am the universe. As long as the universe is there I continue to exist. When the universe is not there I cease to exist." This is not so, for truly reality is birthless and deathless, without self and without other. It does not come and does not depart. It is only by realizing this reality that we can destroy the wrong view of self. Those who simply repeat over and over again "no self" as a religious doctrine have probably lost their way and entered the view of nihilism.

EXERCISE TWENTY-THREE

Being in Touch, Looking Deeply

1. Looking at myself as a five-year-old
child, I breathe in.
Smiling with compassion to the
five-year-old child, I breathe out.

   Myself five years
   old
   Smiling

2. Looking at myself as a
seventy-five-year-old person,
I breathe in.
Smiling to the seventy-five-year-old
person, I breathe out.

   Myself
   seventy-five years
   old
   Smiling

3. Looking at my physical body now,
I breathe in.
Smiling to my physical body now,
I breathe out.

   My body now

   Smiling

4. Aware of the look on my face now,
I breathe in.
Smiling to the look on my face,
I breathe out.

   Look on my face
   now
   Smiling

5. Aware of the state of my skin,   State of skin
   I breathe in.
   Smiling to the state of my skin,   Smiling
   I breathe out.

6. Aware of the state of my hair,   State of hair
   I breathe in.
   Smiling to the state of my hair,   Smiling
   I breathe out.

7. Aware of the state of my heart,   State of heart
   I breathe in.
   Smiling to the state of my heart,   Smiling
   I breathe out.

8. Aware of the state of my lungs,   State of lungs
   I breathe in.
   Smiling to the state of my lungs,   Smiling
   I breathe out.

9. Aware of the state of my liver,   State of liver
   I breathe in.
   Smiling to the state of my liver,   Smiling
   I breathe out.

10. Aware of the state of my bowels,   State of bowels
    I breathe in.
    Smiling to the state of my bowels,   Smiling
    I breathe out.

11. Aware of the state of my kidneys,   State of kidneys
    I breathe in.
    Smiling to the state of my kidneys,   Smiling
    I breathe out.

12. Caring for my heart, I breathe in.   Caring for heart
    Smiling to my heart, I breathe out.   Smiling to heart

13. Caring for my lungs, I breathe in.   Caring for lungs
    Smiling to my lungs, I breathe out.   Smiling to lungs

14. Caring for my liver, I breathe in.   Caring for liver
    Smiling to my liver, I breathe out.   Smiling to liver

15. Caring for my bowels, I breathe in.   Caring for bowels
    Smiling to my bowels, I breathe out.   Smiling to bowels

16. Caring for my kidneys, I breathe in.   Caring for kidneys
    Smiling to my kidneys, I breathe out.   Smiling to kidneys

17. Caring for my brain, I breathe in.   Caring for brain
    Smiling to my brain, I breathe out.   Smiling to brain

This exercise puts us in touch with our bodies and helps us be aware of the condition of each part. It helps us express our concern and our compassion for those parts. This is a form of compassion meditation whose object is the body. It teaches us to live mindfully in order to protect our health and the peace and joy of our bodies. It shows us how to eat, drink, sleep, rest, and work mindfully each day so as not to bring poisons into our bodies. We learn not to work the parts of the body (heart, intestines, kidneys, etc.) to exhaustion, and how to rest, refresh, and restore to each part the capacity to function normally.

EXERCISE TWENTY-FOUR

Looking Deeply

1. Aware of the state of my physical health, I breathe in. Smiling to the state of my physical health, I breathe out.

   Aware of physical health
   Smiling

2. Seeing poisons such as sugar, alcohol, drugs, in my body, I breathe in. Knowing that these poisons are exhausting this body, I breathe out.

   Poisons in body

   Exhausting body

3. Seeing myself bringing poisons such as sugar and stimulants into my body every day, I breathe in. Knowing these poisons are accumulated in my body every day, I breathe out.

   Poisons consumed every day

   Poisons accumulated every day

4. Seeing the necessity for consuming   Consuming
   mindfully, I breathe in.   mindfully
   Determined to consume nourishing   Determined
   foods, and no longer to consume
   physically damaging substances,
   I breathe out.

This exercise goes along with exercise twenty-three. It may help to put a piece of paper and pencil before your meditation cushion and write down what you have determined to do.

EXERCISE TWENTY-FIVE

Looking Deeply

1. Aware of my mental health,
   I breathe in.
   Smiling to my state of mental
   health, I breathe out.

   Aware of mental health
   Smiling

2. Seeing poisons such as anger,
   jealousy, suspicion[1] in my
   consciousness, I breathe in.
   Knowing these poisons are harming
   me and those around me,
   I breathe out.

   Poisons in consciousness

   Harmful to self and others

3. Seeing myself watering these
   poisonous seeds and allowing them
   to be watered every day, I breathe in.
   Knowing that to continue to live like
   this is to add to suffering every day,
   I breathe out.

   Poisons watered every day

   Adding suffering every day

1. Also fear, anxiety, hatred, violence, arrogance, passion, intolerance, illusion, prejudices . . .

4. Seeing myself determined not to water these seeds anymore, I breathe in. Determined to do things like breathing, smiling, and walking mindfully[2], and no longer to do things like judging, blaming, comparing[3], in order to weaken and transform the poisons, I breathe out.

Determined to transform

Acting

This exercise, like the one which precedes it, can also be practiced with the help of pencil and paper. The principle is the same as that of exercise twenty-four. The first stage is to acknowledge the poisons that are already present within us. The second is to recognize the poisons currently being introduced into our bodies and minds. In the third stage, we are able to determine what we should or should not do to transform our state of being.

In the first stage we acknowledge the poisons already present in us: the raw materials of hatred and resentment, fear, violence, infatuation, and anger, which we know are lying in the depths of our consciousness ready to surface at any time to cause us suffering.

In the second stage we acknowledge the evils constantly assailing us during the course of our everyday lives. We are often exposed, if not first hand, then through films, reading material, and conversations, to violence, fear, hatred, meaningless infatuations.

2. Also, listening to, reading, or discussing subjects that can water the seeds of happiness, tolerance, compassion, forgiveness, openness, bringing joy to people . . .
3. Also, listening to, reading, or watching materials that can water the seeds of the poisons mentioned in note 1.

Society is full of violence and hatred, which accumulates in the collective consciousness. If in our daily lives we do not know how to abstain from damaging materials and attitudes, the seeds of violence, hatred, and suffering in us will continue to be watered. We need to be aware of what we hear, see, and read every day. We need to be aware of the cultural products we consume and the people with whom we are sharing experience and conversation. Do our associations and consumptions poison us?

The third stage marks our determination to live in mindfulness to avoid poisoning ourselves anymore. We determine to abandon those things that harm body and mind. We choose which films to watch and which materials to read, and we are careful in the associations we make and the conversations we have. This is not difficult to do if those around us, our families or our communities, are determined to practice together with us. The insights we discover in our meditation can be noted clearly on a sheet of paper. This is a way of establishing a healthy diet for living. By following this diet, we shall be able to restore the health of body and mind and recover joy in being alive. It is best if we can share this exercise with our families or the people with whom we live.

EXERCISE TWENTY-SIX

Looking Deeply

1. Visualizing some damage I have
   done in the past, I breathe in.
   Seeing the suffering I caused in the
   past, I breathe out.

   Damage done

   Suffering caused

2. Seeing my lack of understanding
   while committing the act,
   I breathe in.
   Seeing my lack of mindfulness while
   committing the act, I breathe out.

   Lack of
   understanding

   Lack of
   mindfulness

3. Seeing the past present in me now,
   I breathe in.
   Seeing the wounds of the past
   present in me now, I breathe out.

   Past present in me
   now
   Wounds in me now

4. Seeing the past present in the other
   now, I breathe in.
   Seeing the wounds of the past
   present in the other now,
   I breathe out.

   Past present in the
   other now
   Wounds in the
   other now

5. Saying I am sorry, I breathe in. Determined not to do it again, I breathe out.	Saying sorry Determined not to repeat	1 0 7
6. Seeing that the Five Wonderful Precepts are a protection for me and the other, I breathe in. Determined to practice the precepts deeply, I breathe out.	Protection of precepts Deep practice of precepts	
7. Knowing that by transforming the present, I transform the past, I breathe in. Determined to be mindful and understanding in the present, I breathe out.	Transforming past in transforming present Mindful and understanding now	
8. Smiling to the present, I breathe in. Determined to take good care of the present, I breathe out.	Smiling to the present Taking good care of present	
9. Transforming the past by positive present action, I breathe in. Seeing my present action influencing the future, I breathe out.	Present action transforming past Influencing future	

The purpose of this exercise is to enable us to let go and begin a new life. All of us have made mistakes, have harmed or wounded others, especially those who are close to us. Often we ourselves have been wounded—by our parents, our society, by those we have vowed to love. But we know also that we, because of our lack of understanding and mindfulness, have to a greater or lesser extent caused our own wounds. Moreover, because we lack understanding and mindfulness, we have not been able to transform the wounds that we bear deep within. Above all else this exercise helps us to acknowledge that our injuries are often self-inflicted. When we can acknowledge our responsibility, we will not blame ourselves or feel ashamed, but will instead feel compassion for ourselves and determine to start afresh. The past has not been lost; it has become the present. If we are able to be in touch with the present we are able to be in touch with the past, and if we know how to be responsible for and transform the present we can transform the past. As we shall see in exercise thirty-three, the Five Precepts are not laws to coerce us, but the fruit of mindfulness and an awakened mind. They only protect us and guarantee our own peace, and the peace of others. With the precepts as a foundation, we are immediately able to bring joy once again to others and once again to relieve others of their suffering.

EXERCISE TWENTY-SEVEN

Looking Deeply, Release

1. Contemplating a person in anger,   Angry person
   I breathe in.
   Seeing the suffering of that person,   Suffering
   I breathe out.

2. Contemplating the damage from   Anger harms self
   anger to self and others, I breathe in.   and others
   Seeing that anger burns and destroys   Destroys happiness
   happiness, I breathe out.

3. Seeing anger's roots in my body,   Anger's roots in
   I breathe in.   body
   Seeing anger's roots in my   Anger's roots in
   consciousness, I breathe out.   consciousness

4. Seeing the roots of anger in pride   Anger's roots in
   and ignorance, I breathe in.   pride and ignorance
   Smiling to my pride and ignorance,   Smiling
   I breathe out.

5. Seeing the angry person suffer,
   I breathe in.
   Feeling compassion for the angry
   person who suffers, I breathe out.

   Angry person
   suffers
   Feeling compassion

6. Seeing the unfavorable environment
   and unhappiness of the angry
   person, I breathe in.
   Understanding the causes of this
   unhappiness, I breathe out.

   Angry person
   unhappy

   Understanding
   unhappiness

7. Seeing myself burned by the fire of
   anger, I breathe in.
   Feeling compassion for myself
   burning with anger, I breathe out.

   Burned by anger

   Compassion for
   myself

8. Knowing my anger makes me look
   ugly, I breathe in.
   Seeing myself as the chief cause of
   my ugliness, I breathe out.

   Anger makes me
   ugly
   I cause my ugliness

9. Seeing when angry I am a burning
   house, I breathe in.
   Taking care of my anger and going
   back to myself, I breathe out.

   I am a burning
   house
   Taking care of
   myself

10. Contemplating helping the angry
    person, I breathe in.
    Seeing myself able to help the angry
    person, I breathe out.

    Helping angry
    person
    Capable of helping

The Buddha taught that the fire of anger can burn up everything we have done to bring happiness to ourselves and others. There is not one of us who has not sown seeds of anger in his heart, and if those seeds are daily watered they will grow rapidly and choke us and those around us.

When we are angry, we should come back to ourselves by means of our conscious breathing. We should not look at or listen to the one we feel is making us angry and causing us to suffer. In fact, the main root of our suffering is the seed of anger in us. The other person may have said or done something unskillful or unmindful. But his unskillful words or actions arise from his own suffering. He may just be seeking some relief, hoping to survive. The excessive suffering of one person will very often overflow onto others. A person who is suffering needs our help, not our anger. We come to see this when we examine our anger through our breathing.

Buddha says that anger makes us look ugly. If we are able to breathe when we are angry and recognize the ugliness anger brings with it, that recognition acts as a bell of mindfulness. We breathe and smile mindfully in order to bring some evenness back into our hearts, at the same time relaxing the nervous system and the tense muscles of the face. We must keep on with our conscious breathing as we practice walking meditation in the open air, looking deeply at what has happened. Mindfulness and conscious breathing are sources of energy and can calm the storm of anger, which itself is also a source of energy. If we keep on practicing mindfulness in order to take care of our anger with the affection of a mother when she takes her small child in her arms, then not only shall we calm the storm but we shall be able to find out where our anger really comes from. Our practice, carefully executed, will thus be able to transform the seeds of anger in us.

EXERCISE TWENTY-EIGHT

Being in Touch, Looking Deeply

1. In touch with the flower, I breathe in.   Flower
   In touch with the scent and the   Beauty and scent
   beauty of the flower, I breathe out.

2. In touch with the sun in the flower,   Sun in the flower
   I breathe in.
   Knowing that without the sun there   Without sun no
   would be no flower, I breathe out.   flower

3. In touch with the cloud in the flower,   Cloud in the flower
   I breathe in.
   Knowing that without the cloud   Without cloud no
   there would be no flower,   flower
   I breathe out.

4. In touch with the earth in the flower,   Earth in the flower
   I breathe in.
   Knowing that without the earth   Without earth no
   there would be no flower,   flower
   I breathe out.

5. In touch with the air in the flower,   Air in the flower
   I breathe in.
   Knowing that without the air there   Without air no
   would be no flower, I breathe out.   flower

6. In touch with space in the flower,   Space in the flower
   I breathe in.
   Knowing that without space there   Without space no
   would be no flower, I breathe out.   flower

7. In touch with consciousness in the   Consciousness in
   flower, I breathe in.   the flower
   Knowing that without consciousness   Without
   there would be no flower,   consciousness no
   I breathe out.   flower

8. Knowing that the flower manifests   Flower from six
   from the six elements, I breathe in.   elements
   Smiling to the six elements in the   Smiling
   flower, I breathe out.

9. Seeing the impermanence of the   Flower
   flower, I breathe in.   impermanent
   Seeing the flower on the way to the   Flower turning
   garbage, I breathe out.   into garbage

10. In touch with the garbage,   Garbage
    I breathe in.
    In touch with the impurity and   Impurity and smell
    smell of garbage, I breathe out.

11. In touch with the garbage arising   Garbage from six
    from the six elements, I breathe in.   elements
    Smiling to the six elements in the   Smiling
    garbage, I breathe out.

12. Seeing the impermanence of the
garbage, I breathe in.
Seeing the garbage on the way to
the flower, I breathe out.

Garbage
impermanent
Garbage turning
into flower

13. In touch with the cloud in the
garbage, I breathe in.
Knowing that without the cloud
there would be no garbage,
I breathe out.

Cloud in the
garbage
Without cloud no
garbage

14. In touch with the earth in the
garbage, I breathe in.
Knowing that without the earth
there would be no garbage,
I breathe out.

Earth in the
garbage
Without earth no
garbage

15. In touch with the air in the garbage,
I breathe in.
Knowing that without the air there
would be no garbage, I breathe out.

Air in the garbage

Without air no
garbage

16. In touch with space in the garbage,
I breathe in.
Knowing that without space there
would be no garbage, I breathe out.

Space in the
garbage
Without space no
garbage

17. In touch with consciousness in the
garbage, I breathe in.
Knowing that without consciousness
there would be no garbage,
I breathe out.

Consciousness in
the garbage
Without
consciousness no
garbage

This exercise helps us see the interdependent arising and non-duality of all that is. Interdependent arising is described in the

Avatamsaka sutra as interbeing and interpenetration. We must learn to see the one in the many and the many in the one. Nonduality means that there are not two, but it does not mean that there is only one. The notion one always goes with the notion two and the notion *many*. In comprehending interbeing and nonduality, we will be able to transform our anxieties and fears and to dissolve the barriers of perception that are formed by our habits of conceptualizing and discriminating. The boundaries between birth and death, being and nonbeing, defilement and purity, will be erased, and we will be able to live without fear in the freedom of limitless space.

EXERCISE TWENTY-NINE

Mindfulness of the Awakened One

1. Seeing the Buddha before me in the
seated meditation position,
I breathe in.
Joining my palms in respect,
I breathe out.

Buddha sitting

Joining palms

2. Seeing the Buddha in me,
I breathe in.
Seeing myself in the Buddha,
I breathe out.

Buddha in me

Me in Buddha

3. Seeing the boundary between myself
and the Buddha disappear as the
Buddha smiles, I breathe in.
Seeing the boundary between the
one who respects and the one who is
respected disappear as I smile,
I breathe out.

Buddha smiles, no
boundary

I smile, no
boundary

4. Seeing myself bowing deeply to the
Buddha, I breathe in.

Bowing deeply to
Buddha

This meditation exercise has been applied for more than a thousand years in countries with a Buddhist tradition. In Vietnam, it is used at the beginning of ceremonies before people bow deeply to the Buddha. The traditional wording is: *Since the nature of the one who bows and the one who is bowed to is empty, the communication between us is perfect.* This meditation is rooted in the teachings of interbeing, emptiness, and nonduality. According to the teachings of interdependent arising, both the Buddha and the person who bows before the Buddha are manifested by cause and condition and cannot exist in separation from the rest of all that is. This is what is meant when we say that both are empty. In this context, emptiness means the lack of an autonomously arising, independent entity. In myself are many elements that are not myself, and one of those elements is the Buddha. In the Buddha are many elements that are not the Buddha, and one of those elements is me. It is this insight that enables me to realize the deep contact between myself and the Buddha, and it is this insight that gives the ceremony of paying homage to the Buddha its deepest meaning. It is rare in religious traditions to find this equality between the one who pays homage and the one who is paid homage stated in such an uncompromising way. When we pay homage like this, we do not feel weak or needy. Instead, we are filled with confidence in our capacity to be awakened in the way that the Buddha was.

This exercise can be practiced in sitting meditation or as we bow deeply before the Buddha, Christ, the bodhisattvas, and so on.

EXERCISE THIRTY

Mindfulness of the Awakened One

1. Seeing the Buddha before me,
   I breathe in.
   Seeing myself join my palms in
   respect, I breathe out.

   Buddha before me

   Joining palms

2. Seeing the Buddha before me and
   behind me, I breathe in.
   Seeing myself join my palms and
   bow my head in respect to the
   Buddha before and behind me,
   I breathe out.

   Buddha before and
   behind me
   Joining palms,
   bowing

3. Seeing Buddhas in the ten directions
   as numerous as the sands of the
   Ganges, I breathe in.
   Seeing before each Buddha there is
   an image of myself bowing,
   I breathe out.

   Innumerable
   Buddhas

   One of me bowing
   to each Buddha

This exercise is a continuation of the preceding one. It has also been practiced for more than a thousand years in the Buddhist tradition. The original wording of the exercise goes something like this: *The practice platform which I see before me is the jewelled net of Indra, made of countless precious jewels. All the Buddhas of the ten directions appear reflected in each of the precious jewels and my own image standing before each of the Buddhas is also reflected in each of the precious jewels. As I bow my head before one Buddha I am paying homage to all the Buddhas in the ten directions at one and the same time.* The source of this meditation is the Avatamsaka sūtra. It is based on the principle that one is all and all is one. The exercise helps us to see ourselves beyond the scope of the five aggregates, which are always limited by the framework of space and time. It also helps us to see how we interpenetrate every wonder of our universe.

This exercise, like the preceding one, can be practiced in the sitting position or as we bow deeply.

EXERCISE THIRTY-ONE

Looking Deeply

1. Aware of myself as a collection of five aggregates, I breathe in.
   Seeing the five aggregates rooted in all that is, I breathe out.

   Myself as five aggregates
   Roots in all that is

2. Aware of myself as made up of what is not myself (vapor, water, air, ancestors, habits, society, economics), I breathe in.
   Seeing that my everyday perception of myself as a separate entity is in error, I breathe out.

   Myself made of nonself elements

   Separate entity, erroneous perception

3. Aware of the human species as an animal species though it has a culture and has become sovereign of the earth, I breathe in.
   Seeing that the human species cannot exist without the animal, vegetal, and mineral species, I breathe out.

   Humans one animal species

   No human species without other species

4. Seeing the presence of the human
   species in the presence of the animal,
   vegetal, and mineral species,
   I breathe in.
   Seeing that my idea of myself as
   belonging to a separate, independent
   species is in error, I breathe out.

   Humans in
   animal, vegetal,
   and mineral species

   Seperate species,
   erroneous idea

5. Aware of all animal species as
   subject to birth and death, with
   feelings and consciousness,
   I breathe in.
   Seeing that the animal species cannot
   exist without the presence of the
   vegetal and mineral species, the sun,
   the water, and the air, I breathe out.

   All animal species
   have feelings and
   consciousness,
   impermanent
   No animal species
   without vegetal
   and mineral species

6. Seeing the presence of the animal
   species in the presence of the
   nonsentient species, like plants,
   minerals, sun, water, and air,
   I breathe in.
   Seeing that my everyday perception
   of an animal is in error, I breathe out.

   Animals in
   nonsentient species

   Everyday
   perception of
   animals erroneous

7. Aware of my life beginning at my
   birth and ending with my death,
   I breathe in.
   Seeing that I was already present
   before my birth in many different
   forms and that I shall be present
   when I die in many different forms
   (the sun, the water, the air, the earth,
   ancestors, descendants, habits, society,
   economics), I breathe out.

   My beginning, my
   ending

   No beginning, no
   ending

8. Seeing that my lifespan is not   Life unbounded
   bounded by the span of my birth
   and death, I breathe in.
   Seeing that my perception of a   Lifespan,
   lifespan is in error, I breathe out.   erroneous
                                             perception

This exercise originates in the Vajracchedika Prajñāpāramitā sūtra (known in English as the Diamond sutra), and its purpose is to help us break through our habitual thought patterns, in this case the following four conceptions:

1. The conception of myself as a separately existing entity (parts 1 and 2)
2. The conception of the human species as a separately existing species (parts 3 and 4)
3. The conception of animal species as separately existing (parts 5 and 6)
4. The conception of a lifespan beginning with birth and ending in death (parts 7 and 8)

The quintessent Buddhist teaching is the teaching on emptiness (Sanskrit śūnyatā). Emptiness is a way of expressing that all species exist in connection with and in dependence upon each other. Our meditation practice breaks down the frontiers between us and what seems to be other: the human species and all the other species; the animal species and the so-called nonsentient species; a short lifespan limited by space and time and a lifespan not limited in that way. If we can break through our habitual conceptions and thought patterns, we will emerge in a state of fearlessness, and our love for all species will be like our love for ourselves. Our practice will include the protection of all species, whether vegetable, animal, or mineral. Anyone who works to protect the plants, the animals, the environment of our earth, can take the Vajracchedika sūtra as a fundamental text.

Acting in accord with its teachings, we shall not give way to anger, chagrin, and despair. If we base our actions on perceptions that open wide our mental frontiers, we shall know to use only the materials of understanding and love in our work for all species. In this task, we will feel happy and at peace.

EXERCISE THIRTY-TWO

Looking Deeply

1. Aware of myself picking up an
autumn leaf, I breathe in.
Touching the wonderful
interdependent nature of that leaf,
I breathe out.

   Picking up leaf

   Interdependent
   nature

2. Aware of myself alive here and now,
I breathe in.
Touching the wonderful
interdependent nature of life in me
and around me, I breathe out.

   Alive here, now

   Interdependent life
   in and around me

3. Aware of the leaf returning to the
earth and arising as a new leaf,
I breathe in.
Seeing the leaf in ten thousand
different forms of birth and death,
I breathe out.

   Leaf to earth,
   earth to leaf

   Ten thousand
   different forms

4. Aware of myself as a part of the
   wonderful, interdependent existence,
   I breathe in.
   Seeing that I become manifest under
   many different forms, I breathe out.

   Part of wonderful,
   interdependent
   existence
   Many different
   forms

5. Seeing that the leaf is not really
   born, does not really die, but only
   appears to be born and die,
   I breathe in.
   Seeing that I do not really pass
   through birth and death but only
   appear to, I breathe out.

   Leaf only appears
   to be born and to
   die

   I only appear to
   be born and to die

6. Seeing that the leaf has a
   nirmāṇakāya and functions
   everywhere, I breathe in.
   Seeing that I have a nirmāṇakāya
   and function everywhere,
   I breathe out.

   Leaf functions
   everywhere

   I function
   everywhere

7. Seeing that the leaf has accomplished
   its work from beginningless time,
   I breathe in.
   Seeing that I have accomplished my
   work from beginningless time,
   I breathe out.

   Leaf's work
   beginningless

   My work
   beginningless

8. Seeing that the leaf is already what
   it wants to become, I breathe in.
   Seeing that I am already what I want
   to become, I breathe out.

   Leaf already is

   I already am

9. Seeing that the leaf can call up all its nirmāṇakāyas from beginningless time, I breathe in. Seeing that I can call up all my nirmāṇakāyas from beginningless time, I breathe out.

Leaf's beginningless transformation
My beginningless transformation

This exercise is based on the insights of the Avatamsaka and Saddharmapuṇḍarīka sūtras. In the practice of mindfulness, the meditator can be in touch with the wonderful aspect of reality called the Dharma realm (Sanskrit *dharmadhātu*). Here he will discover that neither he himself nor anything that exists is subject to birth or death. The realm of birth and death is called the world (Sanskrit *lokadhātu*). In the Dharma realm, birth, death, being, and nonbeing do not truly exist. Birth is only an appearance, and the same is true of death. To be born is to appear to be born, and to die is to appear to die. The appearance of a Buddha is not really a new arising: it is just an appearance, like that of an actor on a stage. The life of a leaf too is only apparent. Although it seems to be born and to die, it does not really do so. When it falls from the tree, it is only appearing to pass away, just as a Buddha appears to pass away into nirvana. If a meditator can see this, she will also see that her own birth and death are only apparent. In the Saddharmapuṇḍarīka sūtra (the Lotus sutra), there is a chapter on the lifespan of a Buddha and one on the powers of a Buddha. Someone who has learnt to look at a Buddha in terms of the Dharma realm can see the birthless and deathless nature of the Buddha and realize that Buddha only appears to be born and to die.

The lifespan and the powers of a Buddha cannot be measured.

The lifespan of a leaf and the powers of a leaf are like those of a Buddha, immeasurable. The same can be said of each one of us.

The Saddharmapuṇḍarīka sūtra teaches us to distinguish three dimensions: the historical dimension, the ultimate dimension, and the dimension of action. The historical dimension is the dimension in which we can say that the Buddha is born, is enlightened, teaches The Dharma, and passes away into nirvana. The ultimate dimension is the dimension where Buddha has been Buddha since beginningless time and has been teaching the Dharma and passing away into nirvana since beginningless time. The tower in which Buddha Prabhūtaratna sits—in the Saddharmapuṇḍarīka sūtra, we are told that this tower appears whenever and wherever the teachings of this sutra are given—refers to the ultimate dimension. The Buddha Prabhūtaratna of the past can be touched in the present moment. Sakyamuni Buddha is indeed Prabhūtaratna Buddha. The dimension of action is that of the bodhisattvas, such as Samanta-bhadra, Avalokiteshvara, Bhaishajyaraja, Gadgadasvara and Sadā-paribhūta. All these bodhisattvas voyage in the historical dimen-sion, teaching and helping all beings. Each has been a Buddha since times long past, and from the basis of the ultimate dimension they open up the dimension of action, which means that they appear in the historical dimension, too, for that dimension is the framework for their actions.

If Buddha Sakyamuni and all other Buddhas only appear to come to give the teachings, while in fact their lifespans and their powers are immeasurable, then we can say the same of the leaf and of ourselves.

The Saddharmapuṇḍarīka sūtra shows us that the Buddha is not a lone image arising within the framework of space and time.

The chapter called "Appearance of a Stupa" in the Saddharmapuṇḍarīka shows us that the Buddha has countless transformation bodies arriving in countless worlds to give the teachings. The leaf can also be described this way, as can we ourselves. Each of us has a transformation body in all places, and every action, thought, and word we speak has an influence on the ten directions. This exercise brings us a wonderful concentration. That concentration is called the *saddharmapuṇḍarīka samādhi.*

EXERCISE THIRTY-THREE

Mindfulness of the Precepts

1. Aware of the suffering brought
   about by killing, I breathe in.
   Determined not to kill, not to uphold
   killing or to allow others to kill,
   I breathe out.

   Aware that killing
   brings suffering
   Determined not to
   kill

2. Aware of the suffering brought
   about by exploitation, stealing, and
   injustice in society, I breathe in.
   Determined not to take anything
   which belongs to others,
   I breathe out.

   Aware that
   stealing brings
   suffering
   Determined not to
   steal

3. Aware of the suffering brought
   about by sexual misconduct,
   I breathe in.
   Determined not to engage in sexual
   misconduct, I breathe out.

   Aware that sexual
   misconduct brings
   suffering
   Determined not to
   engage in sexual
   misconduct

4. Aware of the suffering brought
about by unmindful speech,
I breathe in.
Determined to learn to listen to
others and to speak words which are
constructive and bring harmony,
I breathe out.

> Aware that
> unmindful speech
> brings suffering
> Determined to
> listen deeply and
> speak mindfully

5. Aware of the suffering brought
about by alcohol and other drugs,
I breathe in.
Determined not to use alcohol and
other drugs, I breathe out.

> Aware that alcohol
> and drugs bring
> suffering
> Determined not to
> use alcohol and
> drugs

6. Seeing how the Five Wonderful
Precepts protect me, the people
around me, and all species,
I breathe in.
Determined to practice the precepts
for my whole life in order to protect
myself as well as others and all
species, I breathe out.

> Five Wonderful
> Precepts protecting
> me and all other
> species
> Determined to
> practice deeply

The Five Precepts are not prohibitions to restrict our freedom, and they are not an authority which we have no choice but to follow. The precepts are the fruit of our mindfulness and experience. Because we are mindful, we can see that the precepts protect us and our happiness, as well as that of those with whom we live. We take the vow to receive and practice the precepts only because we see the benefits of observing them. We practice the precepts in order to preserve our freedom and happiness in days to come. Being the fruit of mindfulness, the precepts are the embodiment of enlightenment, which is the Buddha himself. They are the embodiment of the Dharma, which is the path shown by the Buddha. They are also the embodiment of the Sangha, the community of all those who have taken up the path. Practicing the Five Precepts is to be one with the Buddha, the Dharma, and the Sangha. To recite the precepts is an exercise in mindfulness of their teachings and a way of looking deeply at the benefits of keeping them. Here follows the ceremony for the reciting of the Five Wonderful Precepts:

RECITING THE FIVE WONDERFUL PRECEPTS

Opening verse:
The Dharma is deep and lovely.
We now have a chance to see it,
study it, and practice it.
We vow to realize its true meaning.

Brothers and Sisters. It is now time to recite the Five Wonderful Precepts. Please, those who have been ordained as Upasaka and Upasika kneel with joined palms in the direction of the Buddha, our teacher.

Brothers and Sisters, please listen. The Five Precepts are the basis for a happy life. They have the capacity to protect life and to make it beautiful and worth living. They are also the door that opens to enlightenment and liberation. Please listen to each precept and answer, "Yes," silently every time you see that you have made the effort to study, practice, and observe it.

The First Precept

Aware of the suffering caused by the destruction of life, I vow to cultivate compassion and learn ways to protect the lives of people, animals, and plants. I am determined not to kill, not to let others kill, and not to condone any act of killing in the world, in my thinking, and in my way of life.

This is the first of the Five Precepts. Have you made an effort to study and practice it during the past two weeks?

(bell)

The Second Precept

Aware of the suffering caused by exploitation, social injustice, stealing, and oppression, I vow to cultivate loving-kindness and learn ways to work for the well-being of people, animals, and plants. I vow to practice generosity by sharing my time, energy, and material resources with those who are in real need. I am determined not to steal and not to possess anything that should belong to others. I will respect the property of others, but I will prevent others from profiting from human suffering or the suffering of other species on earth.

This is the second of the Five Precepts. Have you made an effort to study and practice it during the past two weeks?

(bell)

The Third Precept

Aware of the suffering caused by sexual misconduct, I vow to cultivate responsibility and learn ways to protect the safety and integrity of individuals, couples, families, and society. I am determined not to engage in sexual relations without love and a long-term commitment. To preserve the happiness of myself and others, I am determined to respect my commitments and the commitments of others. I will do everything in my power to protect children from sexual abuse and to protect couples and families from being broken by sexual misconduct.

This is the third of the Five Precepts. Have you made an effort to study and practice it during the past two weeks?

(bell)

The Fourth Precept

Aware of the suffering caused by unmindful speech and the inability to listen to others, I vow to cultivate loving speech and deep listening in order to bring joy and happiness to others and relieve others of their suffering. Knowing that words can create happiness or suffering, I vow to learn to speak truthfully, using words that inspire self-confidence, joy, and hope. I am determined not to spread news that I do not know to be certain and not to criticize or condemn things of which I am not sure. I will refrain from uttering words that can cause division or discord, or that can cause the family or the community to break. I will make all efforts to reconcile and resolve all conflicts, however small.

This is the fourth of the Five Precepts. Have you made an effort to study and practice it during the past two weeks?

(bell)

The Fifth Precept

Aware of the suffering caused by unmindful consumption, I vow to cultivate good health, both physical and mental, for myself, my family, and my society by practicing mindful eating, drinking, and consuming. I vow to ingest only items that preserve peace, well-being, and joy in my body, in my consciousness, and in the collective body and consciousness of my family and society. I am determined not to use alcohol or any other intoxicant or to ingest food or other items that contain toxins, such as certain TV programs, magazines, books, films, and conversations. I am aware that to damage my body or my consciousness with these poisons is to betray my ancestors, my parents, my society, and future generations. I will work to transform violence, fear, anger, and confusion in my self and in society by practicing a diet for myself and for society. I understand that a proper diet is crucial for self-transformation and for the transformation of society.

This is the fifth of the Five Precepts. Have you made an effort to study and practice it during the past two weeks?

> (bell)

Brothers and Sisters, we have recited the Five Wonderful Precepts, the foundation of happiness for the individual, the family, and society. We should recite them regularly so that our study and practice of the precepts can deepen day by day.

Hearing the bell, please bow three times to the Buddha, the Dharma, and the Sangha to show your gratitude.

> Closing verse:
> Reciting the precepts, practicing the way of awareness,
> gives rise to benefits without limit.
> We vow to share the fruits with all beings.
> We vow to offer tribute to parents, teachers, friends, and numerous beings
> who give guidance and support along the path.

EXERCISE THIRTY-FOUR

Prostrating

> With an undivided heart
> To the Buddha, the Dharma, the Sangha
> Which are in the ten directions
> And also in myself,
> Which are in all Dharma realms
> Transcending past, present, and future
> Prostrate and surrendering
> I wholeheartedly go for refuge.

It was pouring rain the morning this gatha was presented for the first time at Plum Village. Before beginning the practice, we sat in front of the large glass doors at the entrance to the meditation hall and watched the rain as it fell to the earth. The gatha may also help you meditate while you prostrate yourself. Like the raindrops, we all must prostrate ourselves. Every one of us is a raindrop, and our earth needs the rain.

You may want to prepare a very clean cloth on which to prostrate yourself. Your face will be in contact with the floor for a longer time than usual, and you do not want to be distracted by the discomfort of breathing in dust.

To prostrate oneself means to flatten oneself. It means you move forward and down at the same time. First you join your palms in front of you. Then a member of the Sangha can read or chant the poem. If you are practicing on your own, you can read it to yourself. On the first, third, fifth, and seventh lines, you breathe in. On the second, fourth, sixth, and eighth lines, you breathe out. Having recited the poem, with a slow, very graceful movement bend down toward the floor. Before placing your knees on the floor, position your hands, one on each side of the place where your head will be. Finally, lower your forehead to the floor. The back of your thighs rests on the back of your shins so that your whole body is close to the floor. Remaining in that position for as long as you want, follow your breath and be mindful of the words of the gatha. You do not have to be mindful of every line if that is too much to concentrate on. One or two lines of the gatha may be sufficient for your meditation.

The ten directions are the eight directions of the compass plus above and below. We say that they contain the Buddha because the Buddha is the awakened aspect of our minds, which can manifest itself anywhere. We do not have to go to Bodhgaya in India to find the Buddha. The Dharma is the teaching about the way things are. If the awakened aspect of the mind is present, then anything can be used to teach us: a flower, a rock, even a harsh word. Sangha is a combination of elements, human and nonhuman, that help us in the practice. The soft grass on which we sit and meditate as well as our friends who sit with us are our Sangha.

Within ourselves as well, we see that every cell contains the

Buddha, the Dharma, and the Sangha. The parts of our bodies that we usually see as clean and those we usually see as unclean are all Buddha, Dharma, and Sangha. Every cell in our bodies contains the earth element, and we prostrate ourselves on the earth. We could not be nearer to the earth and we are not really different from the earth on which we prostrate. In this position, you may experience an overwhelming happiness. Tears may come to your eyes, and you will see that there are many fragrant flowers all around being watered by the rain. Even when the earth seems to manifest no living thing, it contains seeds that may become flowers. Even when you die, as you have done so many thousands of times, a new flower blooms to welcome you home. To prostrate oneself is to die—to die and be happy. Those of you who long to die and shake the red dust of this earth from your feet, you do not have to wait for death to call you. You can surrender yourself right now.

Dharma realms are the objects of our minds. Any element can be the object of our minds and can then be called a Dharma realm. A Dharma realm has something miraculous about it because, though it is phenomenal, it can express the ultimate nature of things. The Buddha, the Dharma, and the Sangha are thus found in everything we can conceive of.

We can transcend past, present, and future. Buddha is not just in the past, in the fifth and sixth centuries B.C.E. Buddha is here with us now, when we know how to be mindful. What were you before you were born as a human being? Were you a cloud before? Buddha was in that cloud. Maybe you were a mosquito and Buddha was in that mosquito. What will you be in the future? Will you be a drop of rain? Buddha, Dharma, and Sangha will be in that drop of rain. We should not think that it is only in this life that we have the capacity to meet the Buddha. We have had many opportunities in the past to be the Buddha, the Dharma, and the Sangha, and we shall have many more opportunities in the future.

In prostrating ourselves, we move down because we are becoming something very humble, and we move forward because we are becoming something very great. We are really nothing, yet at the same time we are in harmony with all the elements in the universe. When you practice a meditation in the prostrate position, you must feel very comfortable. You must surrender and enjoy your conscious breathing. In this position, it is very easy to surrender all thoughts. You can surrender yourself and every thought about yourself. Surrender yourself until you are nothing. This means that there will be no more pride in you. You will not think how intelligent or unintelligent you are, how worthy or unworthy. Pride is a burden we are able to put down when we prostrate ourselves.